MAKE A SCENE

THE REVIEWS ARE IN

"In 'Make A Scene,' Mike has distilled the art of storytelling into a powerful guide—essential for anyone ready to elevate their voice and presence."

— **Joe Russo** | *Emmy Award Winning Director: Arrested Development | Director: Avengers: End Game; Avengers: Infinity War; Captain America: Civil War; Captain America: The Winter Soldier | Academy Award Winning Producer: Everywhere All At Once*

"Mike's infectious energy and wisdom in Make a Scene teach you how to defy gravity and own the spotlight with brains, heart, and courage like a true star"

— **Hayley Podschun** | *Broadway Actress Wicked (Glinda), Hairspray (Tammy) | QVC Guest Host | Keynote Speaker*

"... a refreshing guide to the art of storytelling, anchored in a keen understanding of how we learn and understand the world. A must-read for any leader looking to elevate their communication impact."

— **Hubert Joly** | *Former Best Buy CEO | Senior Lecturer at Harvard Business School | Best-Selling Author, The Heart of Business*

"Mike Ganino takes you beyond just making a scene—he shows you how to steal it, own it, and leave the crowd begging for more. This is the ultimate stagecraft glow-up you didn't know you needed!"

— **Dani Wallace** | *Producer of The BIG Festoon UK and USA*

"'Make a Scene' illuminates the power of authenticity and storytelling, inviting each of us to find our own voice and speak from the heart. It's a transformative guide for leaders ready to inspire."

— **Hortense le Gentil** | *Executive Leadership Coach| Author, The Unlocked Leader*

"Working with Mike made me more compelling, more motivational, more relatable, and more myself."

— **Laura Gassner Otting** | *ABC News Contributor | Wall Street Journal Bestselling Author of Wonderhell and Limitless | 2x TEDx Speaker | #1 Mindset Coach in The World*

MAKE A SCENE

STORYTELLING, STAGE PRESENCE, AND THE ART OF BEING UNFORGETTABLE IN EVERY SPOTLIGHT

MIKE GANINO

authors
AND CO.

First published in 2025
by Authors & Co.
www.authorsandco.pub

ISBN 978-1-915771-96-4 (paperback)
ISBN 978-1-915771-97-1 (hardback)

For Viviana.

I hope you remember to roar when the
world says to stay quiet.
When the world says be small,
you go big.
When the world says simmer down,
you make a scene.
Your voice will always be my favorite,
your stories at the top of my list,
and your full self-expression the greatest
salve in a world gone mad.
Never shrink because someone else is
intimidated by your power.
Papi loves you, chica.

CONTENTS

INTRODUCTION

I know we just met—but if we are going to help you shine in your biggest moments, then we need to get comfortable with each other... and fast.

I challenge you to do something that might feel uncomfortable. Don't worry—discomfort is where growth begins (or so I read on an inspirational social media post once), and I'll be right here with you.

THE CHALLENGE

1. Take out your phone and open the camera app.
2. Set it to video mode and prop it up to face you.
3. Hit record and spend the next sixty seconds introducing yourself:
    a. Briefly explain your personal mission or why you do what you do;
    b. Or share a specific instance when you had to persuade someone to understand or support your mission;
    c. Or describe an experience that has taught you a lesson about how you communicate your ideas.
4. Watch the video back with no audio.
5. Now listen to just the audio without watching yourself.
6. Finally, watch and listen at the same time.

How did that feel? If you're like most people I've worked with—from CEOs to TED speakers, from bestselling authors to quota-busting salespeople—you probably noticed a few things:

- Did your voice sound different than you expected? (You might've cringed listening to yourself and thought, "I can't actually sound like that. Can I?")
- Did you use filler words like "um" and "uh" more than you realized?
- Did your body language feel awkward or unnatural?
- Did you struggle to maintain eye contact with the camera in a way that felt engaging and warm?
- Did the story flow as smoothly as it did in your head, or did it go on some off-road adventures into Rambling-Without-a-Point-Town?
- Did you become the slightly formal, overly "on" presentation version of yourself that loses all the charm you exude when you just talk to someone in front of you?

If you answered yes to any of these, congratulations! You are in great company. Every person I've worked with has had some level of cringe response to that activity—and just like them, you have taken the brave first step toward becoming a more powerful, authentic communicator and away from your communication style holding you back. More importantly, you've just experienced firsthand why this book was designed for you. I am really glad you're holding it.

What is the way you communicate costing you?

FROM SOMMELIER TO STAGE

It is Thursday night in New Orleans. I am nervously finishing the last bites at dinner at the hotel bar and thinking about the keynote I'm supposed to give in the morning. I push my plate away, pay the check, and head up to my room—except, instead of heading up to my room, I head out to the street, to get mugged.

At least, I hoped that was what would happen. Hi, I'm Mike Ganino, and if you have ever felt like your stomach and your brain were fighting a very uncivil war before a speech—one saying it was going to vacate the premises as soon as the other confirmed it was right that everyone in the entire ballroom would stand up in unison and walk out of your talk—then you know what I was feeling that night.

I was due to give my fifth paid speech on Friday morning. The event featured big names like Simon Sinek and Brené Brown, and before that wickedly impresses you, please know that I was on a smaller stage, in a much smaller room, with much smaller font listing my name in the program. So, of course, I thought the perfect Thursday night plan was to wander the streets of the French Quarter with my wallet hanging half out of my back pocket so I could get mugged... you know, mugged just enough to skip my speech without being seriously harmed.

Why? Despite years of experience as an improv performer, corporate trainer, and sommelier, I felt like a fraud. I was following all the "expert" advice, but something was missing. I had done five paid speaking gigs at this point, not to mention twenty or so free ones, hundreds of workshops as a former corporate trainer, and been on handfuls of podcasts. Despite that, I was presenting a version of myself, but it wasn't *me*. It wasn't the vibrant, electric version that people told me they loved off-stage. It was the "presenter" who was trying to be good, trying to be right, trying to be unbothered by the guy in the fourth row with resting bro face.

This disconnect—the gap between who we are and who we think we should be when we communicate—is at the heart of what I do now as a speaking coach and creative director to some of the world's coolest brands, biggest speakers, and most-loved authors. As we will discuss in Chapter 3, this gap is often thinly veiled "impostor phenomenon." The ideas in this book will help you give it the hook. (That's a stage reference to someone being pulled off stage by a hook: get used to references... there are going to be a lot of them around here.)

THE MIKE DROP METHOD: FIVE STAGE LANGUAGES AND RAPID PROTOTYPING

I developed the Mike Drop Method over years of working with:

Corporate clients like

- Walt Disney Company
- Adobe
- Netflix

Non-profits like

- American Cancer Association
- Girls Inc.
- UCLA

Bestselling authors, professional speakers, and TEDx stars like

- Laura Gassner Otting
- Tasha Eurich
- Lori Harder

Ivy League researchers and scientists like

- Harvard's Anthony Jack
- MIT's Erez Yoeli
- Sebastian Buckup from the World Economic Forum

The Mike Drop Method has helped my clients inhabit the most potent and magnetic version of their presence and deliver stories and speeches that have changed their listeners—and the world. In fact, I've trained over 5,000 speakers to help them make a scene. At its core are two key elements that we'll explore in depth in this book:

1. **The Five Stage Languages:** This comprehensive communication model addresses the verbal, vocal, physical, visual, and emotional "languages" we use to connect with our audience, whether on stage, on screen, or in audio. These languages form the foundation of impactful communication, helping you expand your range and make powerful choices that resonate with your audience. This book will guide you through each language and show you how to harness their power for maximum effect.
2. **The Rapid Prototyping Protocol:** This revolutionizes how you prepare and refine your presentations. Unlike traditional rehearsal methods that often lead to stiff, over-memorized performances, the Rapid Prototyping Protocol is a dynamic, playful, and impactful method

for generating ideas, workshopping content, and perfecting your delivery. It teaches you how to iterate quickly, adapt on the fly, and create fresh and authentic presentations every time. This approach helps you refine your delivery, test your content, and perfect your performance to keep your message engaging and your audience captivated.

This method is not designed to turn you into someone you are not—the world doesn't need that! Laura Gassner Otting—Good Morning America/ABC News Contributor, two-time bestselling author, TEDx speaker with over two million views and counting, and frequent media guest—said, "Working with Mike made me more compelling, more motivational, more relatable, and more myself." The Rapid Prototyping Protocol *elevates* your authenticity.

WHY THIS BOOK?

Consider this book your script to help you put your best self on stage, to bring your best ideas to life, and to help you reconnect to the innate, primal energy that makes it impossible for people to take their eyes (and ears) off you so you can share every spark of your remarkable self that your family and friends love. Let's get you fully connected to your stage persona so the world sees the truest version of you. There have been many moments when I didn't show up with my truest truth and it took years of unlearning to break out of the conditioning, minimizing, and shrinking. If you can relate to that, we will get along famously!

This book teaches you to show up authentically by applying the principles of the Five Stage Languages and Rapid Prototyping, whether you're giving a TED talk, pitching to investors, or simply introducing yourself at a networking event. The worst thing you can do is remember all the words and forget the meaning. Your ideas, your story, and your audience are waiting for you to give your communication the spark that starts a movement.

HOW TO USE THIS BOOK

Throughout the book there will be resources and reference materials available at **www.mikeganino.com/bookresources.** You will find links to TEDx talks that we discuss, worksheets to help you with the activities, and some free trainings (like the one about how to keep your voice healthy and strong; or the one about how to organize a speech for maximum transformation).

YOUR TRANSFORMATION STARTS NOW

As we journey through this book together, we'll revisit the video challenge you just completed. The difference in your command of the Five Stage Languages and your ability to rapidly prototype and refine your delivery will amaze you.

My promise to you is that by the end of this book you will have a framework for sharing (and improving) your messages, ideas, and stories in a way that keeps people interested, intrigued, and impacted. How do I know? Because thousands of my clients and workshop attendees have done it and so can you.

Are you ready to master the Five Stage Languages? To transform your nervous energy into a powerful presence? To turn your anxiety into authenticity?

You will soon look back at the video you just recorded (you did just record a video, right?) and barely recognize yourself. You will soon become the communicator you have dreamed of being.

It's showtime.

ACT 1

THE ART AND POWER OF MAKING A SCENE

(OR HOW E.T. PHONE-HOMED HIS WAY INTO MY HEART)

"The function of art is to do more than tell it like it is—it's to imagine what is possible."

— bell hooks

It is one of those rare moments when we can afford cable TV. My single-parent mom is working, and I pretend to be sick so I can stay home from school—a status I master in the years to come as the physical and emotional bullying continues to escalate. Long before the days of choosing what we want to watch from the entirety of the world's content, I'll have to settle on letting the TV tell me what I'll watch within a thirty-two-channel range.

Maury Povich is revealing secret Dads (what a strange prophecy this will become for me). Oprah is not yet giving out cars but addressing the deep narratives of mid-American homemakers. On *El Show de Cristina* the eponymous host is giving her double thumbs up and dropping her classic show-wrapping quote: "Pa'lante, pa'lante; pa'tras ni pa' coger impulso" ("Forward, forward; don't step back, not even to gain momentum"—basically "to get a running start"). Cartoons. An evangelist healing people in a tent. I spin through channels, see people talk about divorce, broken homes, and poverty—none of this is new territory for me, and seeing people fight about it on TV is not of interest. I'm a ten-year-old kid skipping school because the other boys ask him if he's a girl; the teachers give him looks of support that are mostly loosely wrapped pity and barely veiled vicarious embarrassment, and he still feels scared and lost because of his parents' loud and messy divorce.

I'm the only boy in the world going through this.

The clunky, thick rubber button of the remote makes a squishy sound as I click—and then I see him and smile. I say (to no one), "It's been a long time."

It is the end of Act One—Elliott and E.T. have just seen each other for the first time before E.T. runs back into the forest. We already know that Elliott's parents are newly divorced, that he hangs out with his older brother and his friends (instead of having friends his own age), and that his room is messy and not that of a "mature person."

Well—this hits home better than another episode of "I'm cheating on you with my sister, who is secretly also my aunt." I toss the remote onto the blanket on my lap.

If you'd asked me at the time why I liked *E.T.* so much, I would have told you it was because it was one of the first movies I saw in a theater (apparently, the actual first movie I ever saw was 1983's *Flashdance*—an interesting choice for a toddler's first movie—which kind of explains a lot about me and also my relationship with my mom). Even now, I could explain it away with Spielberg's directorial choices, the screenplay's clever devices and dialogue, or the curio cabinet of awards it received (four Oscars, four Grammys, and a massive stack of others). I could even share how it broke *Star Wars'* record for highest-grossing film and held it for eleven years until Spielberg broke his own record with *Jurassic Park* in 1993.

All of that would be a lie.

It was my favorite movie because it made me feel like I was being seen. It helped me feel less alone. In both E.T.—an alien kid left behind—and Elliott—a human kid who felt left behind—I saw something that looked like me. My feelings, fears, and frustrations took form in someone else's story. It was validating, as if somebody had said, "Oh, hey—it's cool to feel how you feel." But also, "Hey, you are gonna be okay, kid," at a time when no one was saying that in my real life.

If I were a betting man, I'd guess you've started thinking about movies from your childhood. Some stories provide a fun escape from reality (although rarely have lasting power), and some give shape, meaning, and significance to the vast ocean swirling around in our guts.

This is the power of storytelling. Our mission is to tell our stories—big and small—as often as possible. Not only do we feel less alone in sharing them, we offer that same solace to others.

In his 2019 TEDxCambridge talk, my client Anthony Jack opens with:

> I remember the first time I stepped foot on the Amherst College campus. It was with my mother and brother. We drove up from Miami—the flights were too expensive and besides, we were all afraid of flying anyway. We pulled up to Pratt Dorm, got out of the car, took deep breaths of fresh country air but then my brother starts to laugh. He saw a little critter run across the yard. He said, "Tony—y'all pay how much for school here and y'all got rats?" Y'all it was a chipmunk. We had never seen a real one before. [My brother's] joke barely hid his excitement—it did nothing for his nerves.
>
> We were in another world.
>
> So—yeah. Me? Here? A Harvard professor in an opera house. It's a testament to the fact that even undreamt dreams come true. I'm the proud son of a middle school security guard, the brother of a janitor—both hard-working but neither college educated. I'm from a poor segregated community in Miami that even my local newspaper called "a place time forgot." There are often more struggles than celebrations. High school was the finish line. When I was growing up, there were only three Ivy League schools: Harvard, Yale, and Princeton and the only reason why Princeton makes the list

> is because of the Fresh Prince of Bel-Air but such is the pernicious power of poverty. It isolates, and it separates. It creates two worlds occupied by the "haves" and the "have nevers." So much so that people equate poor students like myself making it into college as having "made it." The golden ticket—not to Willy Wonka's Chocolate Factory—but to those bastions of power and privilege. Yet getting in is only half the battle.

Anthony was on the Boston Opera House stage to share his "idea worth spreading" based on the research that went into his first book, *The Privileged Poor: How Elite Colleges Are Failing Disadvantaged Students.* And he opened that talk, which has nearly half a million views on YouTube, with the story of his first day on campus. At that point in his career, he had a PhD and a coveted faculty role at Harvard, a published book, and a handful of impressive media features to his name (*New York Times, Boston Globe, The Atlantic*). He stood on the red dot and (as my Granny says) said the truest truth he could think of—his own story.

Your stories have that kind of power. They can light up the dark places, warm those who need comfort, and remind others—and yourself—that you are not alone. They can be the "idea worth spreading" that sparks a movement.

Just like Elliott and E.T. at the end of the movie—standing together, knowing they have to part ways but are forever changed by the connection they've made—your stories will continue to glow, to connect, to resonate long after they've been told.

That is the power of a story. It can make you feel seen, understood, and less alone. It can change your world by showing you that you're not the only one in it. That is exactly what we will explore in this book—how to harness that power of stories in your own communication.

COME ONE
BEHOLD
COME ALL!
OOH!
AHH!
the POWER!!
& the
MAGIC!

CHAPTER 1

THE POWER OF COMMUNICATION

(OR HOW I TRADED TRAILER PARK TWANG FOR OPERA HOUSE OVATIONS)

"Say the truest thing you can."

— Linda Smith (my Granny)

You are standing in front of a room full of people. Your palms are sweaty, your heart is racing, and you're about to deliver a presentation that could make or break your career. You have prepared for weeks, memorized every word, eliminated every "um" and "ah". And yet, as you start to speak, the eyes of your audience glaze over. They are checking their phones, stifling yawns, doing everything but listening to you.

Sound familiar?

I have seen this scenario play out countless times with clients across industries. Take Sarah, for example, a brilliant executive at a major tech company, with ideas that could revolutionize her industry. But every time she stood up to present, she felt she was speaking a different language. Her message didn't land, her passion didn't translate, and her brilliant ideas got lost in translation.

"I have great ideas," she told me in our first session, frustration evident in her voice, "but I just can't get them across. Something's missing when I speak. I want to be more... magical on stage."

Maybe you've felt the same way. Maybe you've tried all the traditional solutions and imagined the audience naked (awkward and not particularly helpful). You have worked tirelessly to eliminate every filler word from your speech only to end up sounding like a well-programmed robot. You have memorized your presentations word for word and spent the entire time terrified you'd forget a line.

And yet, here you are. Something is missing. You are still not making the impact you know you're capable of.

This is the truth bomb I dropped on Sarah, and now I'm dropping on you.

The problem isn't you. The problem is the advice you've been following.

All those traditional public speaking tips and tricks are killing your connection to your audience. They focus on perfection instead of truth, on performance instead of genuine communication. They turn you into a talking head instead of a real, relatable human being.

In other words, they stop you from *making a scene.*

Hear me out. When I say, "make a scene," I don't mean throw a tantrum or cause a commotion. I mean create a moment that matters. A moment that connects. A moment that moves your audience and makes your message stick.

That is what this book is all about: learning to harness the power of authentic communication, crafting messages that resonate, telling stories that captivate, and yes, making scenes that leave lasting impacts.

How do I know this works? Because I've lived it.

I wasn't born into privilege or opportunity—nor the kind of family that produces someone who coaches the smartest thought leaders in the world, is consulted on storytelling by some of the most iconic brands, or writes two books (*Company Culture for Dummies*, 2018, Wiley; and this one!).

Growing up in a small ranch town in California with teen parents, my childhood was a rollercoaster of challenges. When my parents divorced, my little sister and I plunged into poverty with our mom who cleaned houses and did odd jobs to try to make ends meet. The ends rarely met.

At nine, life threw another curveball: a Type 1 diabetes diagnosis. With limited access to medicine and healthy food, managing my health became a daily struggle.

As a "sensitive boy," I faced relentless bullying since elementary school. In middle school, it became so bad that I developed an eating disorder, and social anxiety, and plunged into depression. I ended up in home school to try to save my life. It did—but the bullying followed me into high school.

My journey led me to Chicago as a college dropout, working as a flight attendant—a job that put me on a plane during the fateful events of 9/11. Seeking stability and a job that didn't put me in imminent danger, I became a manager at Potbelly Sandwich Shop, a company I'd stay with as we grew from seven locations to over three hundred in six years. It was here that I discovered my superpower: communication. My ability to connect and convey ideas catapulted my career, leading me to becoming a Director of Training at Potbelly, then a wine educator and Sommelier at Lettuce Entertain You, and eventually a partner and Chief Operating Officer in Protein Bar & Kitchen, a restaurant concept that sold a major stake to a private equity in 2013.

But my true calling was yet to come. I left the restaurant world to pursue a career in speaking and training. Through mastering the art of communication, I transformed from that bullied kid in a trailer park into a trainer and consultant for major brands like Disney, Adobe, Caesars Entertainment, and Netflix; I became Keynote Director to speakers, authors, and thought leaders; I was the Executive Producer of TEDx-NewEngland. Standing on the Boston Opera House stage that hosted our TEDx event felt lightyears away from the broken screen doors and retractable awnings of my youth.

My journey proves that effective communication isn't just a skill: it is a lifeline, a game-changer, and a path to transformation. And now, I'm here to share these tools with you.

This approach has not only transformed *my* life but the lives of countless clients. Like Emily, who went from feeling lost on stage to commanding the room. Or like Chris, a startup founder who used these techniques to secure millions in funding. Or Maria, a non-profit leader who learned to tell her organization's story in a way that doubled donations.

So, are you ready to leave behind the old, ineffective communication advice? Are you ready to stop just speaking and start truly connecting? Are you ready to make a scene?

THE STORYTELLING SUPERPOWER: WHY OUR BRAINS ARE WIRED FOR NARRATIVE

Remember how captivated you felt watching E.T. as a kid? Or maybe it was Star Wars or Toy Story for you? That wasn't just movie magic. It was your brain doing what it does best: connecting with a story.

Our brains are hardwired for narrative. It's not just a preference; it's a neurological fact. When we hear a story, our brains light up like Times Square on New Year's Eve. Research from Princeton University showed that when we're engaged in a story, our brain activity actually synchronizes with the storyteller's – not only in language processing areas, but in any region that would activate if we were experiencing the events ourselves.

In other words, stories don't just entertain us; they transport us. They make us feel. And feeling, my friends, is the secret sauce of memorable communication.

Let me give you an example. I once worked with a client, let's call him Drew, who was struggling to get his team excited about a new company initiative. He had tried presenting the data, showing the projections, explaining the logic. But his team's response was lukewarm at best.

So, we tried a different approach. Instead of starting with numbers, Drew began his next presentation with a story:

"Imagine it's five years from now. You walk into our office, but it's not the office you remember. The energy is electric. At every desk sits someone passionate about what they're doing. On the walls are photos of the lives we've changed with our work. In the break room, people discuss our latest project excitedly. This isn't just a job anymore; it's a movement. And it all started with the initiative we're discussing today."

The result? Drew's team was all in. They weren't just nodding along; they were leaning forward, asking questions, offering ideas. The same information, but presented as a story, had transformed their response.

That is the power of storytelling. It doesn't just convey information; it creates connection. It doesn't just present facts; it paints a picture that people can see themselves in.

This isn't just anecdotal. Studies by neuroscientists have shown that our brains are far more engaged by storytelling than by cold, hard facts. When you tell a story, you're not just communicating; you're creating a shared experience that your audience can more easily recall and remember later.

THE COMMUNICATION CONUNDRUM: WHY SOME MESSAGES STICK AND OTHERS DON'T

Think you don't need storytelling techniques for business presentations? Think again. Whether you're pitching a movie or presenting a budget, the principles are the same. Messages that stick follow the same rules as stories that captivate.

Think about it. What makes a story memorable? It engages our emotions. It creates vivid mental images. It follows a structure our brains find satisfying. Now, what if you could apply those same principles to your business presentations, your sales pitches, your team meetings, and your keynote speeches?

You are going to learn to do exactly that in this book. We are going to turn your data into drama (the good kind), your bullet points into plot points, your information into inspiration.

Because here's the harsh truth: in today's world, being heard isn't enough. You need to be remembered. You need to make an impact. You need to, well, make a scene.

Our lives are mostly about explaining our ideas, our experiences, and our vision—not just having them. It's one thing to have a great idea -- but being able to breathe life into your idea through your communication is the superpower that ignites change.

THE COST OF POOR COMMUNICATION: MORE THAN JUST MISSED OPPORTUNITIES

Let me tell you about Alex. Alex was a brilliant software engineer with an idea that could revolutionize his industry. But every time he tried to explain it to potential investors, their eyes would glaze over. He left meetings frustrated, the investors left confused, and his groundbreaking idea remained just that—an idea.

The cost of Alex's communication struggles wasn't just missed funding opportunities. It was the emotional toll of feeling unheard, misunderstood. It was the gnawing doubt that maybe his idea wasn't as good as he thought. It was the world missing out on an innovation that could have made a real difference. Poor communication isn't just a professional issue -- it's a human one. It keeps us from connecting, from inspiring, from making the impact we're capable of making.

That is why mastering the art of communication—of storytelling, of scene-making—is so crucial. It does not just advance your career (though it will do that). It ensures your ideas are heard, understood, and remembered. It creates connections that can change minds, change lives, and even change the world.

In the coming chapters, you'll dive deep into how to do just that. You will explore the Five Stage Languages to discover your comprehensive toolkit for communication, and unpack the Rapid Prototyping Protocol to transform how you prepare and refine your messages.

Even more than that, you will change how you think about communication. By the end of this book, you won't just be speaking; you'll be storytelling. You won't just be presenting; you'll be performing. You won't just be talking; you'll be making scenes that stick in the minds and hearts of your audience long after you finish speaking.

Are you ready to revolutionize your communication? To turn your messages into memories, your presentations into performances, your talks into transformations?

Then let's start. It is time to make a scene.

COMMUNICATE

SHARE

EVERY DAY

BUILD

STAGES

CHAPTER 2

EVERYDAY STAGES: RECOGNIZING YOUR COMMUNICATION MOMENTS

(OR WHY YOUR STARBUCKS ORDER IS ACTUALLY A TED TALK IN DISGUISE)

> *"All the world's a stage, And all the men and women merely players."*
>
> **— William Shakespeare, As You Like It**

Shakespeare was onto something when he penned those famous lines. Every interaction with other people is an opportunity to make a scene. And I don't mean the kind of scene that gets you escorted out of Target. I'm talking about the kind of scene that leaves an impact, that changes minds, that moves people to action.

THE UBIQUITY OF COMMUNICATION OPPORTUNITIES

Let me tell you about a client of mine. Rachel came to me frustrated. “Mike,” she said, “I’ve been to your workshops. I’ve practiced my presentations. I feel great on stage now. But... it’s not enough. I’m not seeing the career progress I expected.”

“Okay,” I said. “Tell me about your typical day.”

Rachel described her daily routine: the quick chat with her boss in the elevator, the team meeting where she *mostly* listened, the lunch with a colleague, the emails she fired off at the end of the day. I saw the problem. I also saw the opportunity.

“Rachel,” I interrupted, “do you realize you just described at least five ‘stages’ you step onto every single day?”

She looked at me like I’d suggested her coffee mug was actually a shapeshifting alien. “What do you mean?”

“Every single one of those interactions is a chance to make a scene—to communicate your value, to share your ideas, to build relationships. But you’re treating them like they don’t count.”

Rachel isn’t alone. So many of us save our “A game” for the big moments: the presentations, the job interviews, the high-stakes meetings. But here’s a truth bomb: it’s the small moments that add up to big opportunities.

Think about it. When Don Draper in *Mad Men* walks into a room, he’s not just entering a space, he’s making an entrance. Every interaction, from a client meeting to a chat by the water cooler, is a performance. A chance to reinforce his personal brand, to influence, to connect.

Or consider Olivia Pope from *Scandal.* Whether she's advising the President or motivating her team, she's always "on." Every word, every gesture is calculated to achieve her desired effect. She understands that communication isn't just about the big speeches but about the constant, consistent projection of her message and her persona.

Maybe it's even a friend of yours. The one who always seems to know what needs to be said, how to say it, and seems to be fine-tuned to know exactly when to say it. It might seem like an unfair advantage, but it's an advantage that can be learned.

MAPPING YOUR COMMUNICATION LANDSCAPE

How do you recognize these everyday messaging moments? It starts with a simple exercise I call the "Communication Inventory."

Here is how it works:

1. For one full day, carry a small notebook with you (or use a notes app on your phone if you're digitally inclined).

2. Every time you communicate with someone—whether it's a conversation, an email, a text, or even a meaningful look across a room—jot it down.
3. At the end of the day, review your list. For each interaction, ask yourself:
    - What was my goal in this communication?
    - Did I achieve that goal?
    - If not, what could I have done differently?

When I first did this exercise years ago, I was shocked. I had over one hundred distinct communication moments in a single day and I dropped the ball on at least half of them. It was a wake-up call, but also an exciting realization. If I could improve even a fraction of those interactions, the compound effect would be enormous.

And it was. This simple awareness transformed my communication, my relationships, and ultimately, my career. It can do the same for you. What would change in your life with some stronger communication skills? What becomes possible for you? What is it costing you to not invest in your storytelling and stage presence?

MAKING EVERY INTERACTION COUNT

Once you see every interaction as a stage, the next step is to make each one count. This is how:

1. Casual conversations: Stop thinking of small talk as a necessary evil. Instead, see it as a chance to build rapport, to learn something new, to plant the seeds of future opportunities.
2. Professional settings: Whether it's a team meeting or a client call, come prepared with at least one valuable contribution. Don't just attend—participate.
3. Public speaking: Yes, the big presentations matter. But so does the question you ask at a conference, the comment you make in a workshop, the toast you give at a company dinner.
4. Digital platforms: In our connected world, your online presence is a constant stage. That LinkedIn update, that tweet, that email are all chances to reinforce your personal brand and message.

Remember Rachel? Things changed dramatically once she started viewing every interaction as a chance to shine. She contributed more in meetings, used her time with her boss to share her ideas and progress, and turned lunch with colleagues into informal brainstorming sessions.

Six months later, Rachel was promoted. Her boss's reason? "You've really stepped up as a leader in the day-to-day. It's not just your project work: it's how you communicate and inspire the team in every interaction." Talk about #mikedropmoment.

THE BENEFITS OF "MAKING A SCENE"

> *"The stage is not merely the meeting place of all the arts, but is also the return of art to life."*
>
> — **Oscar Wilde**

When you treat every interaction as a chance to make a scene:

1. You stand out in a world of noise. In an age of information overload, consistent, impactful communication makes you memorable.
2. You build a strong personal brand. Your communication style becomes your signature, setting you apart from the crowd.
3. You accelerate your personal and professional growth. Every interaction becomes a chance to refine your message, to practice your skills, to learn and improve.

The effectiveness of storytelling isn't just anecdotal—it's backed by science. A Stanford research study found that stories are up to twenty-two times more memorable than facts alone. Additionally, a study published in *Psychological Science* found that information is more likely to be remembered if presented in a narrative format. These findings underscore the importance of mastering the art of storytelling in your communications.

BREAKING FREE FROM THE STATUS QUO

Some might worry that being "on" all the time could come across as fake or inauthentic. Here's the key: Making a scene doesn't mean putting on an act. It means intentionally bringing your best, most authentic self to every interaction. It's not pretending to be someone you're not—it's being consistently the best version of who you are.

Think of it like this. You wouldn't show up to a job interview in your pajamas, right? You put your best foot forward. Making a scene in everyday interactions works on the same principle. Bring your "A game" to every stage you step on, no matter how small it might seem.

As you read, you'll dive deeper into the techniques and tools to help you make the most of every communication opportunity. For now, start seeing the stages all around you. Once you do, you'll never again look at a casual conversation, a team meeting, or even a text message the same way.

Remember, in the theatre of life, you're not a spectator—you're the star of your own show. Make it a good one. Make a scene worth watching.

Your scene partner awaits.

allow AUTHENTICITY • BE VULNERABLE
RETHINK • YOUR APPROACH •
PREPARATION NOT MEMORIZATION

CHAPTER 3

MYTH-BUSTING AND TRUTH-TELLING: RETHINKING COMMUNICATION ADVICE

(OR WHY "PICTURE EVERYONE NAKED" IS THE WORST ADVICE SINCE "JUST BE YOURSELF")

> *"You wanna fly, you got to give up the thing that weighs you down."*
>
> **— Toni Morrison**

We must put on our myth-busting hats and tackle some of the well-meaning but woefully misguided advice that's been floating around the communication sphere for far too long. Buckle up, because we're about to challenge everything you thought you knew about effective communication.

THE PROBLEM WITH CONVENTIONAL WISDOM

Let me tell you about Tiffany. Tiffany was making waves on the speaking circuit with her expertise in innovation and leadership. Her content was gold—she had the credentials, the case studies, and cutting-edge insights that event planners craved. But despite booking bigger and bigger stages, something wasn't clicking.

Sure, she got polite applause. Decent feedback forms. The LinkedIn connection requests. But she wasn't getting those coveted viral moments, standing ovations, or the holy grail of professional speaking—repeat bookings from word-of-mouth referrals.

Why? Because Tiffany had fallen into the trap that snares so many emerging speakers: she was trying to be what she thought a "professional speaker" should be. She had studied the greats, mimicked their gestures, copied their story structures, and adopted their stage movements. The result? She came across as an impressive but forgettable blend of every other speaker on the circuit.

Tiffany wasn't alone. I've worked with countless speakers who've struggled with the same issue. They come to me with impressive credentials and polished presentations, wondering why their speaking careers aren't taking off despite following all the "expert" advice.

Here's the truth bomb I dropped on Tiffany: Most conventional speaker training advice is, well... garbage. Strong words, I know. But stick with me.

DEBUNKING POPULAR COMMUNICATION TIPS

Let's take a sledgehammer to some of the most common communication myths:

"IMAGINE THE AUDIENCE NAKED."

Whoever came up with this gem clearly never tried it. If you stand on stage and imagine a room of naked people, you will not be focusing on your message. You will be trying not to laugh, cry, or run screaming from the room.

Try this instead: Imagine the audience as allies, as friends who want you to succeed. Because guess what? They do. Nobody shows up to a presentation hoping the speaker will bomb. Your job is to connect and communicate directly to them – not think of them in their Calvin's (which is honestly creepy advice, right?).

"ELIMINATE ALL YOUR 'ISMS' AND QUIRKS."

This advice turns vibrant, unique self-expression into lukewarm oatmeal. Your quirks, your "isms" are part of what makes you, you. They are part of your charm, your authenticity.

Embrace your uniqueness. Polish it, refine it, but don't eliminate it. Your quirks are your trademark, your brand. Use them wisely, intentionally, and as an asset.

"DUMB DOWN YOUR MESSAGE."

This one makes me want to bang my head against a wall. Your audience isn't dumb. They don't need you to "dumb down" your message; they need you to make it clear, relevant, and engaging.

Focus on making your message accessible. Use stories, analogies, and examples to illuminate complex ideas. Don't dumb it down; light it up.

"ELIMINATE ALL FILLER WORDS."

While it's true that too many "ums" and "ahs" can distract an audience, obsessively eliminating every single filler word can make you sound robotic and over-rehearsed.

Instead, focus on the flow of your speech. A few natural pauses or filler words can make you sound more human, more relatable. Aim for balance, not elimination.

RETHINKING STORYTELLING ADVICE

Now, let's tackle some storytelling myths:

"EVERY STORY NEEDS A CLEAR BEGINNING, MIDDLE, AND END."

While structure is important, a rigid adherence to linear storytelling can kill the natural flow and authenticity of your story. Some of the most impactful stories start in the middle, flash back to the beginning, or leave the end open for interpretation.

Focus instead on the emotional journey of your story. What do you want your audience to feel? How can you take them on that journey most effectively?

"FORCE YOUR STORY INTO THE HERO'S JOURNEY FRAMEWORK."

The hero's journey is a powerful storytelling tool, but it's not the only one. Trying to force every narrative into this structure can make your stories feel formulaic and predictable.

Let the natural structure of your story emerge. Sometimes, the most powerful stories are the ones that break the mold.

THE TRUTH ABOUT GREAT COMMUNICATION

So, if all this conventional wisdom is wrong, what's right? It's certainly not a rigid dogma about how something as creative, emotional, and subjective as public speaking and storytelling. Here is the truth:

Authenticity trumps perfection

Your audience doesn't want a perfect, polished robot. They want a real, relatable human being. Embrace your authenticity, quirks and all.

Vulnerability creates connection

Don't be afraid to show your human side. Share your struggles, your doubts, your failures. Vulnerability isn't weakness; it's the ultimate strength in communication.

Preparation doesn't mean memorization

Being prepared doesn't mean reciting a script word-for-word. It means knowing your material so well that you can adapt it on the fly, respond to your audience, and stay present in the moment.

THE ANATOMY OF A STELLAR COMMUNICATOR

What does a great communicator look like? They are:

1. **Honest:** True to themselves and their message.
2. **Empathetic:** Able to connect with and understand their audience.
3. **Adaptable:** Flexible enough to adjust their communication style as needed.
4. **Present:** Fully engaged in the moment, not just reciting memorized lines.

Cultivating these qualities doesn't mean following a set of rigid rules. It means developing your unique voice, understanding your audience, and constantly refining your approach.

INTRODUCING A NEW PARADIGM FOR COMMUNICATION MASTERY

> *"Language is wine upon the lips."*
>
> — **Virginia Woolf**

This is where the Five Stage Languages and the Rapid Prototyping Protocol come in. These aren't one-size-fits-all solutions. They are flexible frameworks that allow you to develop your own communication style.

The Five Stage Languages—verbal, vocal, visual, physical, and emotional—give you a comprehensive toolkit for communication. They allow you to craft messages that don't just inform but resonate on a deeper level.

The Rapid Prototyping Protocol revolutionizes how you prepare and refine your communication. It doesn't depend upon rote memorization or rigid structures. It is about iterative improvement, constant refinement, and adapting to your audience in real time.

As we dive deeper into these concepts in the coming chapters, keep one thing in mind: The goal isn't to turn you into some idealized version of a "perfect communicator." The goal is to help you become the most authentic, impactful version of yourself.

The ultimate truth about great communication is that it's not about being perfect. Great communication is about being real, being present, and yes, being willing to make a scene.

Are you ready to break free from the shackles of conventional wisdom? To embrace your unique voice? To do the kinds of things that change minds, touch hearts, and maybe even change the world? I knew you'd say "yes."

ACT 2

FIVE STAGE LANGUAGES

(OR HOW TO BECOME A POLYGLOT OF MAGNETIC PRESENCE)

"I want to stand as close to the edge as I can without going over. Out on the edge you see all kinds of things you can't see from the center."

— Kurt Vonnegut

My heart raced as I read the email of every speaker's dreams:

"We would love to have your help again this year with our annual General Manager conference."

It was from a major US hotel group for whom I'd keynoted the previous year. Repeat clients are the holy grail in this business, a sign you've truly nailed it. My excitement grew as I read on.

"Our teams are still talking about the story you shared about working with your Grandma at Pizza Hut," she continued. I couldn't help but smile. That keynote, which focused on how company culture is about the stories people in our business tell, had been a hit. It was right before I published my first book, *Company Culture for Dummies* (yes, one of those famous "Dummies" books).

But then came the twist: "We have already booked our speakers for this year's event..."

My heart sank for a moment, but I kept reading.

"... and we really need our executive team to step it up in their speeches this year. We all agreed it would be great to hire you to coach them on how to dazzle the audience like you did last year. Can we talk about what it would look like to hire you to help them be 'more like Mike' as one of our VPs put it."

I sat back in my chair, a mix of excitement and panic washing over me. Of course, I was going to say yes—it was a huge brand and an incredible opportunity. But I had no clue how to help someone "be more like Mike." Hell, I wasn't entirely sure what I was doing when I did it, let alone how to recreate it on demand.

I had been keynote speaking up to now about company culture and the stories we tell at work, delivering workshops and consulting on leadership and HR topics. Sure, I'd occasionally throw in ideas from my work as an improv performer (something I later learned is called "Applied Improvisation"). But how was I going to help a bunch of stiff executives loosen up, connect through storytelling, and generate the kind of stage presence that engaged a group of overworked and ambitious hotel managers?

That is when it hit me—I needed a system, a framework to break down the magic of great communication into learnable, repeatable elements. So began my deep dive into the world of public speaking.

I studied and analyzed about five hundred of the best TED talks, keynote speeches, and media interviews on YouTube, trying to dissect what the person on "stage" was doing and how someone else could replicate it authentically. Patterns began to emerge, and the Five Stage Languages were born.

What I discovered was this: Perfect communication isn't just about what comes out of your mouth. It is a full-body sport that engages your intellect, voice, senses, body, and emotions. It is the difference between a monotone lecture that puts people to sleep and a riveting performance that has your audience on the edge of their seats, hanging on your every word.

Enter the Five Stage Languages: Verbal, Vocal, Visual, Physical, and Emotional. Think of these as your communication superpowers. They are the secret sauce that turns a good talk into an unforgettable experience. They are the difference between being forgettable and being legendary.

Let's take a page from the master storyteller himself, Steven Spielberg. The guy doesn't just tell stories; he creates entire worlds that suck you in and don't let you go until the credits roll. Every word of dialogue, every note of music, every visual cue, every actor's movement, every emotional beat—it's all carefully orchestrated to create a complete experience. He doesn't leave anything to chance.

Remember the soaring music in *E.T.* that made your heart swell? That is vocal language at work. The stark visual contrasts in *Schindler's List* that spoke volumes without a word being uttered? That is Spielberg's visual language doing its thing. The visceral, gut-wrenching battle scenes in *Saving Private Ryan* that made you feel the cost of war in your bones? Those are the physical and emotional languages tag-teaming to knock your socks off.

Minus the multi-million dollar special effects budget, that's exactly what we're aiming for.

You might be thinking this all sounds a bit dramatic. After all, you're not trying to win an Oscar—you just want to give a great talk, tell some relatable stories, and maybe earn a standing ovation. Fair enough. This isn't about turning you into an actor or going for an Emmy Award-winning performance (unless that's your thing, in which case, go for it—and don't forget to thank the little people). This is about helping you make authentic choices that align with your true self, and expand your range in each of these languages so you can express yourself more fully and connect more deeply.

Whether you're speaking to a boardroom of ten or a ballroom with ten thousand people at the Bellagio Resort in Vegas, these Five Stage Languages are your ticket to connection, impact, and yes, even a bit of razzle-dazzle.

Think of it this way: Your talk is a conversation with the audience. Yes, you read that right. Not a monologue, not a lecture, but a dialogue. The audience is your scene partner, and you must be in constant communication with them, even when they don't say a word.

You might think that since they came to hear you speak, you should be doing all the talking. Well, yes, but also no. If you ignore your scene partner (the audience), you're not having a dialogue; you're just having a very public conversation with yourself. And trust me, no one wants to watch that.

This is where the Five Stage Languages come in. They are your tools for keeping that dialogue alive and kicking, even if it's the twentieth time you've given this talk this month. (If that's the case, kudos to you, you speaking superstar!)

Let's address the elephant in the room: the dreaded stage fright. You know, that feeling that makes you want to control every little thing about yourself on stage. "*Control your hands. Control your head. Control your voice.*" Sound familiar? But here's the dirty little secret: trying to control everything is exactly what holds you back.

When we say someone has "stage presence," what we really mean is that their communication is clear, direct, efficient, and emotionally engaging. They have cleared away all the junk that stops them from fully expressing themselves. Your body is an instrument for expression, not containment. This is why it feels weird on stage when you're not open—the expression is limited.

Your job is to expand the range of choices you can make on stage. To break free from the habitual ways of expressing yourself you've developed over the years. To notice your ways of being and find ways to expand that range. To try new things to see if they can become part of your toolkit.

The chapters that follow dive deep into each of these Five Stage Languages. You will learn how to craft words that stick, use your voice like a finely tuned instrument, create visuals that enhance rather than distract, move with purpose and grace, and tap into the emotional core of your message.

But remember, these languages aren't separate entities. They are the Avengers of communication—each powerful on its own, but unstoppable when they work together. These languages intertwine and reinforce each other to create a communication experience greater than the sum of its parts.

By the end of this section, you'll have a powerful storytelling toolkit that allows you to connect with your audience on every level, leaving a lasting impact long after you've left the stage. Great storytelling isn't just what you say; it's *how* you say it, *show* it, and make your audience *feel* it.

So, are you ready to unleash your communication superpowers?

Alchemy
HUNT
BUILD
CRAFT
ADAPT
MASTER

CHAPTER 4

THE VERBAL LANGUAGE AND STORYTELLING ALCHEMY: TURNING LIFE'S LEAD INTO NARRATIVE GOLD (OR HOW TO MAKE "PASS THE SALT" SOUND LIKE SHAKESPEARE'S LOST FOLIO)

> *"Your experience is your only real currency. The only thing you can really bring to the table that's going to make you different from anyone else is what you've lived through and what you've learned from it."*
>
> — **Taylor Swift**

It is 2009, and I'm in Washington, D.C., opening a new Home-Made Pizza Company location—a bougie take-and-bake pizza place where I'm the Director of Operations. My life is a whirlwind of expansion plans and relationship drama—oh, to be twenty-nine. I pull into the restaurant's parking lot and the DJ announces a new song from Taylor Swift. This is still in her curly hair more country than pop days so I start to get out of the car. Then the opening guitar licks catch my ear. It sounds fun and upbeat. As the lyrics to "You Belong With Me" rock along, I'm hit with a pang of recognition so strong that I'm glad I stayed in the driver's seat.

How did this girl I've never met manage to capture exactly how I feel? How did she write the exact specific storyline I am living out? And why am I always the one sitting on the bleachers? (That's a song reference, for you non-Swifties.)

That, my friends, is the power of storytelling.

In just a few lyrics, Taylor Swift had painted a picture that resonated with millions, including yours truly. That is what you'll learn to do in this chapter—minus the guitar, record deal, and friendship bracelets (sorry, folks).

Welcome to the storytelling workshop, where we'll turn your experiences into narratives that captivate, inspire, and maybe even change a few lives along the way. If you think you don't have any stories worth telling, trust me, you do. We just need to dig them out, polish them up, and present them in a way that makes people lean in and say, "Tell me more!"

This chapter is all about the Verbal Stage Langauge. This is about the actual words, stories, and phrases you tell on stage. It draws inspiration from master storytellers across various fields from TED stages to Broadway theaters, from Madison Square Garden to keynotes at the Hilton Garden Inn. You will see how great orators, writers, even pop stars, use narrative techniques to connect deeply with their audiences on an emotional level.

The goal isn't to turn you into the next Shakespeare or Taylor Swift (although if that happens, I expect a shout-out in your Grammy speech). It is to help you find the most authentic, impactful way to tell your stories. At the end of the day, it's not about crafting perfect prose—it's about creating genuine connections.

So, if you are ready to turn your experiences into stories that resonate, inspire, and maybe even change the world a little bit, let's start crafting those narratives. After all, every great story starts with a single moment: you have a lifetime of moments just waiting to be told.

THE STORY HUNT: MINING FOR YOUR STORIES

Grab your pickaxes and hard hats, storytelling prospectors. We are going digging for narrative gold in the mine of your experiences. Trust me, there's a motherlode in there waiting to be discovered.

You might think you need to have climbed Everest or won a Nobel Prize to have stories worth telling. Here's the truth: some of the most powerful stories come from everyday moments. I call these "It Happened on a Tuesday" stories.

Story Hunt 1: The Five-Second Moment of Change

This is the secret sauce of great storytelling: It is not about grand, sweeping epics. Find those tiny moments when everything shifted, even if you didn't realize it at the time.

Think about it. Was there a moment when you made a small decision that changed the course of your life? Maybe you chose a different route to work and bumped into your future spouse. Perhaps you decided to speak up in a meeting, leading to a career-altering project.

These are your five-second moments of change. They are the pivot points in your life story: they're storytelling gold.

Action:

The Moment Mining Challenge

1. Set a timer for five minutes.
2. Write down as many "moments of change" as you can remember. They don't have to be huge, just times when something shifted, even slightly.
3. For each moment, jot down:
    - What happened just before;
    - The moment itself (in as much detail as you can);
    - What changed after.

Story Hunt 2: The Personal Touch: Making Every Story About You

Sometimes the stories we need to tell aren't directly about us. Maybe you need to talk about your company's history or explain a complex concept. Every story can (and should) be personal.

Let's say you need to talk about your company's new sustainability initiative. Boring, right? But it won't be if you start with why it matters to you. Maybe you remember the first time you saw a sea turtle tangled in plastic, or perhaps you are inspired by your kid's passion for recycling.

By connecting the story to your personal experience, you make it relatable and give your audience a reason to care.

Action:

The Personal Connection Finder

1. Think of a "non-personal" topic you need to discuss (e.g., a work project, a historical event, a scientific concept).
2. List three ways this topic connects to your personal experiences or values.
3. Draft an opening sentence that bridges your personal connection to the larger topic.

Story Hunt 3: Anecdotes vs. Stories: Know the Difference

A common pitfall is confusing anecdotes with full-fledged stories. An anecdote is a brief, often amusing account of an incident. A story has a beginning, middle, end, and most importantly, a point.

For example:

> **Anecdote**: "I once saw a guy try to parallel park for twenty minutes straight. It was hilarious!"
>
> **Story**: "I once spent twenty excruciating minutes watching a guy try to parallel park. As the line of cars behind him grew, so did my empathy. I realized how often we judge others without considering their struggles. It changed how I approach patience in my daily life."

See the difference? The story takes the anecdote and gives it meaning, connecting it to a larger theme or lesson.

Action:

From Anecdote to Story

1. Write down a brief anecdote from your life.
2. Now, expand it into a story by asking:
   - What was the context?
   - How did it make you feel?
   - Did it change your perspective on something?
   - What larger truth or lesson can be drawn from this experience?

Story Hunt 4: The End Game: Know Where You're Going

Before you start crafting your story, it's crucial to know where you're heading. What point are you trying to make? What do you want your audience to feel or do after hearing your story?

A clear endpoint will help you structure your story effectively, ensuring every detail serves a purpose.

Action:

The Endpoint Definer

1. Choose a story you want to tell.
2. Write down:
   - The main point or lesson of the story;
   - How you want your audience to feel;
   - What action (if any) you want your audience to take.
3. Now, work backward. What details must you include to reach this endpoint effectively?

Remember, storytelling isn't about recounting every detail of what happened. Curate the most impactful moments and weave them together to create meaning. As you mine for your stories, always ask: What's the gold here? What's the nugget of truth or insight that will resonate with your audience?

In the next section, we'll dive into how to take these raw materials and craft them into compelling narratives. But for now, happy hunting! Your best stories are out there, waiting to be discovered. They are probably hiding in the most unexpected places—like a rented Toyota Camry in a restaurant parking lot with a Taylor Swift song on a random Tuesday in 2009.

SOURCE MATERIAL: PUTTING YOUR STORY TOGETHER

Now that you've unearthed your narrative gems, it's time to polish them into something shiny. But before we break out the storytelling jewelry kit, we've got to talk about storytelling frameworks.

The Framework Fallacy

You have probably heard of the Hero's Journey, the Three-Act Structure, or any number of other storytelling frameworks. And sure, they can be useful. But here's a hot take for you: sometimes, these frameworks are about as helpful as a chocolate teapot.

Real life doesn't always fit neatly into pre-packaged structures. Some of the most powerful stories out there break all the "rules." So instead of trying to cram your unique experiences into someone else's mold, focus on what really matters: authenticity and impact.

That said, I won't leave you hanging. Here is a more flexible approach to putting your story together:

The Beat Sheet: Your Story's Stepping Stones

Think of your story as a journey across a river. The beats are the stepping stones that get you (and your audience) from one side to the other. They are the key moments that move your story forward.

Action:

The Beat Sheet Breakdown

1. Take the story you want to tell.
2. List out the key moments or "beats" in bullet point form. Don't worry about order yet, just get them all down.
3. Now, arrange these beats in an order that feels natural and builds tension or interest.

   For example, let's break down my Taylor Swift parking lot epiphany:
   - Arriving at work, feeling stressed about expansion plans;
   - Hearing the opening chords of a new song;
   - Recognizing my own feelings in the lyrics;
   - Realizing the power of storytelling in connecting people.

See how each beat moves the story forward? That is what we're aiming for.

Scene Setting: Lights, Camera, Action!

Once you have your beats, turn them into vivid scenes. This is where you transport your audience right into the moment with you.

The key question here is. "If I was filming this, what would I be shooting?" What's in frame (a cinema term for "what is getting picked up by the camera"? Who's there? What are you experiencing?

Action:

What's in Frame?

1. Take one beat from your story.
2. Close your eyes and imagine you're there again. What do you see? Hear? Smell? Feel?
3. Write a description of the scene, focusing on sensory details and your internal experience.

   For example:

   "I grip the steering wheel, my palms slightly sweaty from the D.C. summer heat. The radio DJ's voice cuts through my mental to-do list. 'And now, the new single from Taylor Swift!' Guitar chords fill the car, and suddenly, I'm not thinking about pizza dough or expansion plans. I'm transported back to high school, to unrequited crushes and the ache of not fitting in."

Stay Active in the Scene

This trips up a lot of people. They start telling the story from the outside, like they're narrating a nature documentary about their own life. But we want to keep things active and immediate.

> Instead of saying, "I was nervous standing in front of the hiring committee," try something like:
>
> "I rub my hands on my pant legs, trying to wipe off the sweat before I shake their hands. My stomach is doing somersaults; my brain is trying to sabotage me, and I pray I remember how to speak when my presentation starts. 'You really need this job, Mike,' I keep reminding myself."

See the difference? We feel every nervous twitch right there with you. When people say "show, don't tell" in reference to storytelling – this is what they mean. Show us what being nervous was like – don't just summarize it.

The Inner Monologue: Welcome to My Brain

One of the most powerful tools in your Verbal Stage Language toolkit is the inner monologue. This is where you let your audience in on what's happening inside your head. Don't just tell us what happened; tell us how you felt about it, what you were thinking, what you were afraid of. This is how the real connection happens.

Action:

The Stream of Consciousness

1. Choose a significant moment in your story.
2. Set a timer for two minutes.
3. Write non-stop, capturing every thought and feeling you had in that moment. Don't censor yourself; let it all out.
4. Review what you've written and highlight the most impactful or revealing thoughts. These are gold for your story.

Remember, putting your story together doesn't mean following a rigid structure. Find the most compelling way to take your audience on a journey with you. Make them feel what you felt, see what you saw, and understand why this moment mattered.

In the next section, you will look at different ways to structure your story for maximum impact. But for now, focus on bringing those key moments to life. Make them so vivid that your audience forget they're listening to a story and start feeling like they're living it with you.

And hey, if you manage to make them feel like they're sitting in a car in 2008, having an existential crisis to a Taylor Swift song, you know you've nailed it. Let's keep exploring the Verbal Stage Langauge by looking at storytelling structures.

STRUCTURING YOUR STORY: BUILDING YOUR NARRATIVE ARCHITECTURE

You are about to construct some narrative skyscrapers that'll have your audience gazing up in wonder. But don't worry—we're not going all fancy with Victorian gargoyles and flying buttresses. We are aiming for storytelling structures that are rock-solid yet flexible enough to adapt to any tale you want to tell.

The Chronological Approach: Just the Facts, Ma'am

Sometimes, the simplest approach is the most effective. The chronological structure is exactly what it sounds like—telling your story in the order it happened. It is straightforward, easy to follow, and incredibly powerful when done right.

Let me take you back to 2008, to a story that illustrates this beautifully. I am backstage at Chicago's Museum of Contemporary Art, volunteering for Art Smith's Common Threads' Third Annual World Festival. Thanks to my friendship with Amanda Puck, a celebrated Chicago food publicist and one of the event chairs, I find myself on grunt duty, stuffing gift bags like my life depends on it.

Suddenly, the bustling backstage area falls silent. I look up, wondering if I've missed some sort of "quiet on the set" cue, only to find myself face-to-face with Padma Lakshmi, the event's mistress of ceremonies. I met my fair share of celebrities in my restaurateur days, but Padma? She has that elusive "x-factor" in spades. It isn't that she demands silence in that "don't look her in the eyes" kind of way—her mere presence is enough to hush a room.

As she approaches, I can't help but notice her famous scar—the one that has been a talking point throughout her modeling and TV career. But in this moment, it is just another facet of her striking appearance. What really catches me off guard is her warmth and humor. She cracks a joke so delightfully inappropriate that I find myself thinking, "Did the most beautiful woman in food media really just say that?"

Fast forward two years to 2010. I am sitting in the audience at The Moth NYC Mainstage, and guess who's taking the stage? Padma Lakshmi. She begins her story, "That Thing on My Arm," and I am transported back to that moment backstage in Chicago. But this time, I am about to learn the story behind that famous scar.

Padma's story unfolds like a perfectly paced novel. It begins with a hospital visit to diagnose a rare illness, moves to her mother's promise to make a penance if Padma is released from the hospital okay, then to her stepfather driving them to the temple, and finally to the car accident that gave her the scar. Each event leads naturally to the next, creating a narrative that is easy to follow yet utterly captivating.

This, my friends, is the power of chronological storytelling. By presenting events in the order they occurred, Padma created a clear path for her audience to follow. We were right there with her, experiencing each moment as it unfolded, building tension and emotional investment with each new development.

The chronological approach works because it mimics how we experience life—one moment at a time, each building on the last. It creates a natural sense of progression and allows the audience to connect cause and effect easily. Plus, we're all inherently familiar with this structure, making it accessible to any audience.

Even within this straightforward structure, Padma managed to create suspense and emotional resonance. She didn't just recite a timeline of events; she crafted each moment to reveal character, build tension, and ultimately, deliver a powerful message about self-acceptance and resilience.

The next time you're crafting a story, consider the chronological approach. It might seem simple, but in the hands of a skilled storyteller, it is a powerful tool for creating connection, building suspense, and delivering unforgettable narratives. Just remember—whether you're talking about a life-changing scar or last night's dinner, it's not just about what happened, but how you tell it.

The Flashback: Back to the Future (or Past)

The flashback structure starts your story at a critical moment, then jumps back in time to show how you got there. It is like narrative time travel, and when done well, it creates instant intrigue.

Think about how many movies start with an intense scene, then hit you with the "24 hours earlier" title card. It works because it immediately hooks your audience and makes them curious about how things led to that point.

Action:

The Time Jump

1. Identify the most dramatic or intriguing moment in your story.
2. Write a brief, vivid description of this moment.
3. Now, think about where the "real" beginning of your story is.
4. Practice transitioning from your dramatic opening to this earlier starting point.

The James Bond: Shaken, Not Stirred

This structure is a variation on the flashback but with a twist (much like 007's favorite drink). You start at a critical moment, flash back to tell the chronological story, then return to that opening scene and continue forward. It's like serving your audience a storytelling sandwich—a dramatic opening and closing as the bread, with the meaty details in between.

Let me show you how this works through a story I helped my long-time client Erin King reshape. Her original version started chronologically with her grandmother's marriage to "Wild Bill" Faulkner, moved through his funeral, and ended with her using one of his sayings in a make-or-break investor meeting.

To transform it into the James Bond structure, we reordered the elements to create more tension and anticipation:

1. We opened in the middle of her pitch meeting: "I stare across the shiny conference table, the Pacific Ocean sparkling out the window—waiting on a bunch of CrossFit Ferrari dudes to decide my fate." We established the stakes immediately: maxed-out credit cards, last shot at making her dream work.
2. Just as the investors are about to give their verdict, we hit pause. We flash back to Wild Bill's funeral, where young Erin learned about his way of turning strangers into opportunities, including the pivotal phrase "Smart people bet on the jockey, not the horse."
3. Then we return to that conference room, where Erin, channeling her grandfather's spirit, delivers the perfect response to skeptical investors: "Well, I guess it all comes down to whether you're the kind of investor who bets on the jockey or the horse."

This structure is one of my favorite devices to use with keynote speakers because it holds a live audience's attention so perfectly. The key is to keep the scenes very easy to understand by not having too many locations—notice how it wasn't Erin at home worried about her business, Erin driving to a meeting, Erin walking up to a conference room. It was the boardroom and the funeral. Even Wild Bill's time at the bar was still inside of the "funeral" in the audience's mind. This helps the audience not get confused by this story with a cliff-hanger opening.

The result? Instead of a linear progression, we created a story that hooks the audience immediately, builds anticipation, and delivers a satisfying payoff. The same events, shaken and stirred, become much more engaging.

Finding the Beginning: The Origin Story

The beginning of your story isn't always where you think it is. To find the true starting point, ask yourself, "When was my life/belief/experience the opposite of where I ended up?"

This creates a clear arc of transformation, which is what great stories are all about. It sets up the essential question for your audience: How did you get from A to B?

Action:

The Opposite Game

1. Write down where your story ends—the final state, belief, or situation.
2. Now, think back to when things were the complete opposite.
3. This is your true beginning. Start your story here.

**DIRECTOR'S CUT:
STOP DRY HUMPING THE AUDIENCE**

I'm working with my client Abhi on his "Burn the Bat" story. He's giving me all the backstory. And I mean *all* of it. We're talking family history, childhood memories, what he ate for breakfast that day—everything except the actual bat-burning moment we're supposedly heading toward.

Finally, I had to step in with what has become one of my signature phrases: "Stop dry humping the audience."

Look, I get it. You want to set the scene. You want your audience to understand every nuanced detail that led to your big moment. But here's the thing: Too much exposition is like making out with your audience for three hours and never getting to the good stuff. You're exhausting them before you even reach the point.

Your audience doesn't need your protagonist's entire life story to care about what happens next. They need you to get closer to where something actually happens. You've got about sixty seconds before they start checking their phones—so instead of starting with your grandfather's immigration story, start with "I was standing in my backyard holding a bat, lighter fluid, and my ex's favorite memories." Now *that's* a beginning that makes people lean in.

Here's the magic: Starting closer to the action doesn't mean telling a shorter story. Your twelve-minute story is still a twelve-minute story—but instead of spending half of it clearing your storytelling throat with exposition, you can use that time for the juicy stuff. Let us feel your sweaty palms as you grip the bat. Share your inner monologue about whether revenge really does smell like lighter fluid. Give us those rich, vivid details of being in that moment rather than a history lesson about how you got there. Your audience will thank you for it.

Quick & Dirty Rule: Start as close to the action as possible while still maintaining emotional impact. If you're more than sixty seconds from something happening, you're probably dry humping your audience. Your story won't be shorter—it'll just be sexier.

GPS + Calendar Invite: Pinpointing Your Story

Every great story needs a specific location (like a GPS dot on a map) and a specific time (like a calendar invite). You might never mention the exact date in your story, but knowing it helps ground your narrative in reality.

This specificity turns a vague anecdote into a vivid scene, the difference between "I once had a job interview" and "On a sweltering August morning in 2015, I found myself in the glass-walled lobby of Acme Corp, sweating through my only suit."

Action:

The Time and Place Anchor

1. For each main scene in your story, write down:
   - The exact date (even if it's just your best guess);
   - The specific location;
   - One vivid sensory detail about that time and place.
2. Use these anchors to add depth and authenticity to your story.

The Vonnegut Shapes: Universal Story Arcs

Kurt Vonnegut, the literary genius who could make you laugh and cry in the same sentence, proposed that stories tend to follow certain emotional arcs. While we're not big on rigid frameworks, these shapes can be useful tools for understanding the emotional journey of your story. Let's break them down:

1. **Rags to Riches (rise)** This is your classic "zero to hero" story. You start at the bottom and end up on top. Example: *Slumdog Millionaire* or Oprah Winfrey's life story.
2. **Riches to Rags (fall)** The opposite of the above. You start high and end low. It is not the happiest arc, but it can be powerful. Example: *Breaking Bad* or the story of Bernie Madoff.
3. **Man in a Hole (fall then rise)** You're trucking along, then bam! You hit a low point. But don't worry, you climb back out. Example: Pretty much every sports movie ever made, or my personal journey through the 2008 financial crisis.
4. **Icarus (rise then fall)** Named after the Greek myth, this is when you soar too close to the sun and then plummet. Example: *The Wolf of Wall Street* or the rise and fall of many tech startups.
5. **Cinderella (rise then fall then rise)** You get a taste of the good life, lose it all, then gain it back (usually with some hard-earned wisdom). Example: The actual *Cinderella* story, or many comeback narratives in music and sports.
6. **Oedipus (fall then rise then fall)** This is the roller coaster nobody wants to ride. You hit a low, recover, then plummet again. Example: The tragic arc of

Oedipus in Greek mythology, or many stories of addiction and relapse.

Vonnegut also identified two more shapes that are worth mentioning:

7. **Which Way Is Up?** This is for stories where it's hard to tell if things are getting better or worse. It's all about perspective. Example: *Catch-22* or the movie *Eternal Sunshine of the Spotless Mind.*
8. **Creation Story** This starts low, shoots up, then levels off. It is the classic "And then things were good forever" ending. Example: Many religious creation myths or the founding stories of successful companies.

Ready to try this out? Here's a quick exercise:

Action:

Shape Shifter

1. Think of a personal story you want to tell.
2. Sketch out its emotional arc on a piece of paper. Don't overthink it, just go with your gut.
3. Compare your sketch to Vonnegut's shapes. Which one does it most closely resemble?
4. Now, try reimagining your story in the shape of a different arc. How does this change the emphasis or impact of your story?

These shapes aren't about forcing your story into a mold. They are tools to help you understand the emotional journey you're taking your audience on. Sometimes, the most powerful stories are the ones that subvert these expected arcs. This is the Verbal Stage Language at its best.

The key is to be conscious of the emotional arc you're creating. Are you taking your audience on a steady climb to triumph? A series of ups and downs? A dramatic fall with a phoenix-like rise from the ashes? Whatever shape you choose, make sure it serves your story and the impact you want to have on your audience.

In the end, the best shape for your story is the one that feels true to your experience and resonates with your audience. So don't be afraid to draw outside the lines. After all, you're not just telling a story—you're creating an emotional experience.

In the next section, you'll figure out how to organize and write your story down. But for now, play around with these different structures. Try telling your story chronologically, then as a flashback, then as a James Bond. See which feels most natural, which creates the most intrigue, which best captures the essence of your experience.

And remember, no matter which structure you choose, make sure it feels as authentic and lived-in as a favorite pair of jeans. Because the best stories aren't just told—they're experienced.

ORGANIZING AND WRITING YOUR STORY: FROM BRAIN TO PAGE

It's time to take that rough block of narrative marble and chisel it into a masterpiece. This means moving from the realm of ideas into the nitty-gritty of getting your story down on paper (or screen, for you digital Michelangelos out there).

Storyboarding: Your Story's Comic Book

Remember those beat sheets we talked about earlier? Well, it's time to level up. Go full Hollywood and storyboard your tales. Don't worry, you don't need to be a Pixar-level artist for this.

Storyboarding means visualizing your story in a series of scenes or moments. It is like creating a comic book version of your narrative. This technique helps you see the flow of your story and identify gaps or pacing issues.

Action:

The Sticky Note Storyboard

1. Grab a stack of sticky notes and a pen.
2. On each sticky note, sketch (stick figures are fine!) or write a key scene from your story.
3. Arrange these notes on a wall or large piece of paper in the order of your narrative.
4. Step back and look at your story as a whole. Are there gaps? Does the flow make sense?

5. The beauty of sticky notes is that you can rearrange them. Play around with the order until it feels right.

There is a moment in all my private coaching days or in-person retreats when I draw a series of boxes on the whiteboard and then help to draw some quick images inside them. The images correspond to beats or moments of my client's story. Then they stand up and try to tell the story based on the images in the boxes. It looks a little like a comic book—if comic books were made by people with little drawing talent. This trick almost always helps them remember the story and tell it in a more scenic way. Win-win.

Stage to Page: Speak Before You Write

Here is a counterintuitive tip: before you start writing, start talking. I call this the "Stage to Page" method, and it's a game-changer for creating natural, engaging narratives.

Most people speak differently than they write. When we write, we tend to get formal, using clunky sentences and big words we'd never use in conversation. But when we speak, we're more natural, more authentic, and often more engaging.

Here is how to do it:

1. Set up a voice recorder (your phone probably has one built-in).
2. Pretend you're telling your story to a friend over coffee. Just speak naturally, as if you're having a conversation.

3. Record yourself telling the story several times. Each time, you'll likely remember new details or find better ways to explain things.
4. Listen to your recordings and transcribe the best parts.
5. Use this transcript as the basis for your written story, maintaining the natural flow and authenticity of your spoken words.

This method helps you avoid slipping into "presenter mode" or sounding too formal. It keeps your writing conversational and relatable.

Action:

The Coffee Shop Confessional

Find a quiet spot (or an actual coffee shop if you're feeling brave), set up your recorder, and tell your story as if sharing it with a close friend. Don't worry about getting it perfect—the goal is to capture your natural speaking style and the organic flow of your narrative.

The Magic of Editing: Less Is More

Earlier, we talked about how memorizing a story word-for-word can make it feel stiff and rehearsed—we want your stories to feel lived, not recited. But here's a seemingly contradictory piece of advice that's actually complementary: writing your story down can be incredibly valuable for the editing process.

Think of it like a chef's recipe. Even if you eventually cook by feel, having a written recipe helps you refine the ingredients and proportions. The same goes for your story. A written version gives you a concrete starting point for editing, serves as a memory trigger before performances, and lets you track how your story evolves over time.

So let's put on our editor's hat. And let me tell you, it should be a hat with "Less Is More" emblazoned across the front.

Editing isn't just about fixing grammar and typos (though that's important too). It means honing your story to its sharpest, most impactful form. Here's how:

1. Cut the fat: If a sentence, paragraph, or even a whole section doesn't serve your story's main point, be ruthless. Cut it out.
2. Tighten your language: Look for places where you can say the same thing in fewer words. It isn't about using big words; it's about using the right words.
3. Read it aloud: This helps you catch awkward phrasing and ensures your story maintains a natural, conversational flow.
4. Get feedback: Share your story with trusted friends or colleagues. Fresh eyes can spot things you've become blind to.

Remember, your first draft is you telling the story to yourself. Editing is about crafting it for your audience.

Action:

The Ruthless Revision

> Take a draft of your story and challenge yourself to cut it down by twenty-five percent. Yes, it's painful. Yes, it feels like you're killing your darlings. But trust me, your story will be leaner, meaner, and more impactful for it.

The Final Polish: Making It Shine

Once your story is structured, spoken, written, and edited, it's time for the final polish. Make sure every word earns its place, every sentence flows into the next, and your story sings. The appendix in the back titled: *The Art of Rhetoric: Wordplayers Gonna Play, Play, Play, Play, Play (or How to Make Your Words as Catchy as a Taylor Swift Bridge)* also has a bunch of great little flavor-boosting tricks that will make everyone crave your words.

Here are some final touches to consider:

1. Strong opening: Does your first line grab attention and set the tone?
2. Satisfying ending: Does your conclusion tie everything together and leave a lasting impression?
3. Sensory details: Have you included enough vivid details to bring your story to life?
4. Emotional journey: Does your story take the audience on an emotional ride?

5. Authenticity check: Does it sound like you? Does your unique voice shine through?

Remember, the goal isn't perfection. The goal is impact. If your story connects with your audience and leaves them feeling something, you've nailed it.

The impact of strong communication skills on professional success cannot be overstated. Research from Harvard Business Review shows that strong communicators are thirty-four percent more likely to receive high performance ratings. Furthermore, a study by MIT's Human Dynamics Laboratory found that communication patterns were the most important predictor of a team's success. Clearly, investing in your communication skills pays dividends in the workplace.

The next section talks about how to adapt your story for different contexts and audiences. But for now, focus on getting your story out of your head and onto the page in the most authentic, impactful way possible. Your story matters, and the world is waiting to hear it.

ADAPTING YOUR STORY: ONE TALE, MANY TELLINGS

It is time to flex those adaptation muscles. Just like a chameleon changes its colors to fit its environment, a great storyteller adapts their tale to fit different contexts. After all, the story you tell at a TED Talk probably shouldn't be the exact same one you share at your cousin's wedding (unless your cousin is really into professional development, in which case, rock on).

Know Your Audience: The Golden Rule of Adaptation

Before you start tweaking your tale, you need to know who you're tweaking it for. Understanding your audience is like having a secret map to their hearts and minds. Here's what to consider:

1. Demographics: Age, profession, cultural background, etc.
2. Knowledge level: Are they experts in your field or complete newbies?
3. Expectations: What do they hope to get out of your story?
4. Context: Is this a formal presentation, a casual chat, or something in between?

Action:

The Audience Avatar

> Create a detailed profile of your target audience. Give this imaginary listener a name, a background, and specific interests. Then, as you adapt your story, ask yourself, "Would [Audience Avatar Name] connect with this?"

A few years into my speaking career, I did an event for Zingerman's in Ann Arbor, Michigan. I was speaking about using ideas from improv theater to create better teams through the stories they tell about work, and in the audience were a few people who worked at public libraries. They must've liked it because I booked ten gigs with Michigan- and Ohio-based public libraries in the twelve months that followed. This gave me the chance to create a new story to open my talk about being a poor thirteen-year-old boy living with my mom and sister in a trailer and using the Escondido Public Library to escape and learn about the world.

Laura Gassner Otting did this beautifully when she was hired to speak at the same venue she had gotten married at twenty-five years before. She weaved that into her speech for luxury wedding planners and even put a picture of the exact room she was speaking in taken the night it was transformed for her wedding reception. She does not normally talk about this—but what a pro move to customize her keynote in this way.

Tailoring Your Tale: The Art of Customization

Once you know your audience, tailor your story. This is how to customize your narrative without losing its essence:

1. Adjust your language: Use terms and references your audience will understand and appreciate.
2. Emphasize relevant parts: Highlight the aspects of your story that will resonate most with this specific group.
3. Adapt your examples: Choose analogies and illustrations that fit your audience's experiences.
4. Modify your tone: Match the level of formality or casualness to the setting.

Remember, adapting your story isn't about changing its core truth. It means finding the most effective way to connect that truth to your specific audience.

Action:

The Story Remix

> Take your core story and adapt it for three different audiences (e.g., a group of CEOs, a classroom of fifth graders, and your grandmother). Notice how the essence stays the same, but the delivery changes.

Time Constraints:
The Incredible Shrinking (or Expanding) Story

Sometimes, you've got an hour to tell your story. Sometimes, you've got thirty seconds. Being able to expand or contract your narrative is a crucial skill.

For longer formats:

- Add more sensory detail and context.
- Include additional anecdotes that support your main point.
- Delve deeper into the emotions and thought processes involved.

For shorter formats:

- Focus on the most crucial turning point.
- Use vivid, concise language.
- Cut to the chase—what's the key takeaway?

Action:

The Elevator Pitch

> Craft a thirty-second version of your story. What absolute essence do you need to convey? Now expand it to two minutes, five minutes, and ten minutes. Notice how you decide what to add at each stage.

Incorporating Your Story Into Larger Presentations

Your story doesn't always have to be the main event. Sometimes, it's a powerful tool within a larger presentation. This is how to weave your narrative into a broader context:

1. Use it as an opener: A personal story can be a great way to grab attention from the start.
2. Illustrate a point: Your story can serve as a real-world example of a concept you're explaining.
3. Provide a breather: In the middle of data-heavy content, a story can re-engage your audience.
4. Close with impact: End your presentation with a story that ties everything together.

Remember, your story should serve your overall message, not overshadow it.

Want to craft a knockout keynote? I've got something special for you tucked away in the appendix: my ***Transformational Narrative framework***. This three-act, nine-part model doesn't just help you build speeches—it creates experiences that transform your audience right there in their seats (yes, even in the Des Moines Marriott ballroom). Don't just take my word for it—New York Times bestselling author and TEDx sensation Tasha Eurich (she's racked up over 9 million views) puts it this way: "Since I've started speaking in 2007, I feel like I have a keynote that gives me permission to fully be myself on stage."

Action:

The Story Integration Challenge

> Take a presentation you've given before (or create a simple one on a topic you know well). Find three places where you could potentially integrate a personal story. How would each placement change the impact of your presentation?

The Bottom Line: Flexibility Is Key

The art of adapting your story requires flexibility. Holding on to the heart of your narrative while being willing to shift the delivery to best serve your audience and context.

Your story is like water. The essence remains the same whether it's in a tiny shot glass or a giant water cooler tank. Your job is to be the container that shapes the water for each specific situation. Find new ways to make your core story resonate in any situation; don't create a new story for every situation. Master this, and you'll be able to connect with any audience, anytime, anywhere.

Our last section of the Verbal Stage Language explores some practical exercises to help you hone all the storytelling skills we've covered. But for now, start thinking about how you can adapt your story for different contexts. After all, the best stories aren't just told once—they're told again and again, each time in a way that feels fresh, relevant, and impactful.

PRACTICAL EXERCISES AND TECHNIQUES: YOUR STORYTELLING GYM

It's time to hit the narrative gym. So far, we've been working with individual storytelling elements—like a fitness enthusiast practicing specific movements. We've mined for raw story material, learned how to shape our stories for different audiences, and picked up techniques to make them more engaging. These were all essential building blocks.

Now we're ready to put these pieces together into complete, powerful stories. Think of these next exercises as your full-body workout routine for storytelling. Instead of isolating specific skills, we'll be crafting stories from start to finish, using everything we've learned. They might make you sweat a little, but I promise you'll come out stronger on the other side—with stories that can actually move and inspire an audience.

The Story Spine: Building Your Narrative Skeleton

Kenn Adams—author of *How to Improvise a Full-Length Play: The Art of Spontaneous Theater*—created a simple story structure to help improvisers quickly craft a story, making sure it hits all the dopamine-boosting plot points while keeping the story moving forward.

The Story Spine is a simple but powerful tool for structuring your stories. It goes like this:

1. Once upon a time... this section sets up the basic information we need to know to make sense of the world the story is taking place in.
2. Every day... this part establishes the status quo, sets up the "old normal" of the story.

3. But one day... something changes, and sets the character (you!) into motion.
4. Because of that... now delve into the consequences of that thing happening.
5. Because of that... do further into the consequences of the last "because of that" happening.
6. Because of that... one more for good measure—each of these relates to the last "because of that" and *not* to the original "but one day" change.
7. Until finally... this is the emotional high of the story; the turning point; you make a critical choice that changes us and gets us your "happily ever after".
8. And ever since then... this establishes the new status quo; shows us the transformational from the opening scenario.

This structure works for everything from fairy tales to business presentations. It gives you a clear beginning, middle, and end, with built-in turning points.

Example from *The Wizard of Oz*:

1. Once upon a time there was a little girl named Dorothy who lived in Kansas with her Auntie Em and Uncle Henry and her dog, Toto.
2. Every day, she was bored and ignored in her daily life on the farm.
3. But one day, a tornado came and twisted her away to a magical place called Munchkinland where she is told that in order to get home she must meet the Wizard of Oz by following the yellow brick road.

4. Because of that, she met a Scarecrow, a Tin Man, and a Cowardly Lion who all needed help from the Wizard, too, and agreed to accompany her while she wore the magical ruby slippers of the Wicked Witch of the East that she landed on.
5. Because of that, the Wicked Witch of the West sent her monkeys to kidnap Dorothy and Toto so she could get her sister's shoes back.
6. Because of that, the three travel partners come to rescue Dorothy and the Scarecrow's arm is lit on fire by the Witch.
7. Because of that Dorothy threw water on him which splashed the Witch and melted her away.
8. Because of that she got the Witch's broom that the Wizard of Oz had requested in order to help Dorothy return home.
9. Because of that, the Wizard agreed to take Dorothy home in his hot-air balloon.
10. Until finally, on the day of their departure, Dorothy ran after her dog, Toto, and missed the balloon.
11. And ever since then, Dorothy learned that she always had the power to get home on her own, which she did.

In this example, you can see how each "scene" (or beat) added another "because of that" along the way—and how each "because of that" caused the next one to happen. This keeps the story moving, shows cause and effect, and keeps the audience engaged.

Action:

The Story Spine Workout

1. Choose a personal experience or a business case study.
2. Fill in each line of the Story Spine with a sentence from your chosen story.
3. Flesh out each sentence into a paragraph.
4. Read your story aloud. Does it flow naturally? Does it hit all the key points?

The Verb Upgrade Challenge: Powering up Your Language

Verbs are the engines of your sentences. Upgrading your verbs can dramatically enhance the impact of your story.

Action:

Verb Vivification

1. Write a short paragraph about a significant moment in your life.
2. Highlight all the verbs.
3. For each verb, brainstorm at least three more dynamic alternatives.
4. Rewrite your paragraph using the most vivid, specific verbs.

For example, instead of, "I walked into the room," you might say, "I strutted into the room," or, "I slouched into the room," depending on the mood you want to convey.

The Dialogue-Only Story: Mastering Conversation

Dialogue can bring your stories to life, making them more engaging and relatable. This exercise helps you focus on creating authentic, revealing conversations.

Action:

The Silent Movie Script

1. Choose a key moment from your story.
2. Write it using only dialogue—no description, no "he said/she said."
3. Make sure each line of dialogue reveals character, advances the plot, or both.
4. Read it aloud with a friend, each taking different parts.

This exercise forces you to make every word count and helps you develop distinct voices for different characters.

The Five Senses Challenge: Creating Vivid Scenes

Great storytellers engage all the senses, making their audience feel like they're right there in the moment.

Action:

Sensory Overload

1. Choose a setting from your story.
2. Write five sentences, each focusing on a different sense (sight, sound, smell, taste, touch).
3. Combine these sentences into a vivid paragraph that brings your setting to life.

You don't always need all five senses, but considering each one can help you find the most evocative details.

The Emotion Swap: Flexing Your Adaptation Muscles

This exercise helps you practice adapting your story for different emotional impacts.

Action:

The Mood Ring

1. Write a brief version of your story with a specific emotional tone (e.g., inspirational, humorous, suspenseful).
2. Now, rewrite the same story with a completely different emotional tone.
3. Compare the two versions. What changed? What stayed the same?

This exercise helps you see how the same events can be framed differently to create different emotional responses in your audience.

The Pitch Perfect Challenge: Adapting for Time Constraints

Being able to tell your story in different time frames is crucial for any storyteller.

Action:

The Shrinking Story

1. Grab the phone and tap that camera button.
2. Hit record and tell a five-minute version of your story. Stop recording.
3. Now do a 2.5-minute version—same story; same insight; same transformation.
4. And now a one-minute version.
5. Finally, create a thirty-second version.

This exercise helps you identify the core of your story and practice adapting it for different situations.

> Bonus: this is one of the activities I do in my Mike Drop Era Retreats by grouping together three people. Person one does step one and two; the second person does step three by shrinking the original person's story; then the third person does step four based on what they just heard; it finally comes back to the original storyteller to complete step five.

The Improv Infusion: Embracing Spontaneity

Improvisation skills can make your storytelling more dynamic and help you adapt to unexpected situations.

Action:

The Random Word Integration

1. Ask a friend to give you three random words.
2. Tell a story you know well, but you must incorporate these three words seamlessly.
3. Reflect on how this changed your story. Did it lead to any new insights or angles?

This exercise helps you think on your feet and find unexpected connections in your stories.

Remember, these exercises are not about perfection. They are about exploration, growth, and finding new dimensions to your storytelling. The more you practice, the more natural and powerful your storytelling will become.

In the words of the great Ira Glass, "The most important thing you can do is do a lot of work. Do a huge volume of work. Put yourself on a deadline so that every week or every month you know you're going to finish one story. It's only by going through a volume of work that you're actually going to catch up and close that gap."

In the end, the best shape for your story is the one that feels true to your experience and resonates with your audience. So don't be afraid to draw outside the lines. After all, you're not just telling a story—you're creating an emotional experience.

And if you're sitting there thinking your story isn't dramatic enough, exciting enough, or interesting enough to warrant all this architectural attention, remember this: ***There is no such thing as a boring story. Only a storyteller who has yet to find the truth.***

Because the best stories aren't just told—they're excavated. They're unearthed. They're discovered in the moment you realize why that memory keeps tugging at your sleeve, why that scene plays on repeat in your mind, why that seemingly simple moment changed everything. These structures? They're just your shovels and brushes for the dig.

Your stories are waiting to be told, and with these Verbal Stage Language tools in your belt, you're ready to tell them better than ever. But before we move along to the second of the Five Stage Languages, I want to help you tickle your audience's funny bone. Nothing makes an audience fall in love with a presenter like a good laugh.

CHAPTER 4.5

HOW TO FIND THE HUMOR (WITHOUT MAKING PEOPLE WISH YOU'D CHOSEN MIME AS A CAREER)

"I succeed by saying what everyone else is thinking."

– Joan Rivers

Aspiring comedians and accidental clowns, gather 'round. We are about to embark on a journey into the treacherous world of humor. But fear not! This isn't about turning you into the next Jerry Seinfeld (although if that happens, I expect a cut of your Netflix special). This is about finding the funny in your everyday communications without making your audience cringe so hard they pull a muscle. This section is an expanded part of the first of the *Five Stage Languages:* Verbal before we move along to the second of the languages: The Vocal Stage Language.

THE GOLDEN RULE: FIND HUMOR, DON'T FORCE FUNNY

Here's something liberating: You don't need to be "funny" to use humor effectively. Professional comedians work in a pressure cooker where success is measured in laughs per minute. But as speakers and storytellers, we're playing a different game entirely. Our goal isn't to deliver a rapid-fire string of punchlines—it's to find those universal human moments that make people nod and smile in recognition.

Humor is your secret weapon. It's the WD-40 of communication, smoothing out rough patches and making everything work better. When you capture a truth about everyday life that everyone has noticed but no one has named, you create an "aha moment" that connects deeply with your audience. Their brains light up like Christmas trees, dumping feel-good chemicals that make them like you more, trust you more, and even think you're smarter (it's a neat trick, even if you're not).

The bar for using humor in a speech isn't nearly as high as you might think. You don't need perfect timing or snappy one-liners. You just need to share honest observations about the absurdities we all live with but rarely discuss in a way that surprises the audience. Let me show you few ways to get started.

THE LUCILLE BALL EFFECT

"I'm not funny. What I am is brave."

— Lucille Ball

Fun fact: In the corporate world, the bar for humor is so low, you could trip over it (don't even get me started on things like commencement speeches and wedding toasts – both things I have worked on with clients). Even a slight chuckle can win you the "Lucille Ball Humor in Conference Room B Lifetime Achievement Award." (Still bitter I never got that one when I was teaching restaurant managers about implicit bias. Their loss.) "I'm here to help you clear the low bar with ease. To figure out how to be funny, you need to understand what humor is and how it works.

WHAT MAKES SOMETHING LAUGHABLE?

Here are some ingredients of humor, and before you fault me for missing one that your favorite huckster mentioned once during a Netflix special please know this list isn't exhaustive:

1. Surprise: This is the classic setup-punchline structure. We expect X, we get Y, and suddenly milk is coming out of our noses.
2. Anticipation: When the audience starts to see where you're going before you get there, like watching a car crash in slow motion... but funny.
3. Empathy: The "OMG, we've all been there" moment. Like when I talk about my daughter evolving from a sweet two-year-old into a "threenager" who told

me she, "doesn't like my face today." (True story. Still hurts.)

4. Contrast: Push two different things together and watch the sparks fly. It is the "straight man vs. funny man" dynamic that's been making people laugh since vaudeville.

The Secret Sauce: Surprise

At the end of the day, all humor in speaking, storytelling, and social media comes from surprise. It is about subverting expectations, zigging when everyone expects you to zag.

WHEN TO USE HUMOR

1. In the first minute: Nothing makes an audience fall in love with you faster than tickling their funny bone.
2. Before/after heavy content: It gives everyone an emotional breather.
3. When you need to up the stakes but are fresh out of ideas. It is like a humor defibrillator for your audience's attention span.

WHERE TO FIND HUMOR

Lists:

- Unexpected items in a list;
- Exaggerated lists;
- Lists that start normal and end absurd.

Example: "Things I need for this presentation: my laptop, my notes, a fire extinguisher, and the collective willpower of a thousand caffeinated squirrels."

Examples:

- Extreme or absurd examples;
- Personal, relatable examples;
- Unexpected twists on common examples.

Example: "Our new software is so user-friendly, even my technologically-challenged grandma could use it. And trust me, this is a woman who once tried to make a phone call on a calculator."

Anecdotes:

- Self-deprecating stories;
- "Fish out of water" experiences;
- Unexpected outcomes.

Example: "The first time I tried to impress my in-laws, I decided to cook a gourmet meal. Three fire alarms and one visit from the local fire department later, we ordered pizza."

Delivery:

- Unexpected pauses;
- Exaggerated facial expressions;
- Comedic timing (we'll dive deeper into this in the voice and physicality sections).

Example: "And then I said... [long pause, deadpan expression] ... no."

STRATEGIES FOR GETTING LOLZ

Callbacks:

- Reference earlier jokes or comments;
- Create a running gag throughout your presentation;
- Use callbacks to tie different parts of your talk together.

Example: If you mentioned struggling with technology earlier, later you might say, "And then I finally figured out how to use the new software. It only took three IT professionals, a psychic, and a small animal sacrifice."

Heightening:

- Exaggerate size, degree, intensity, quality, or importance;
- Start with a relatable situation and gradually make it more extreme;
- Use the "Rule of Three": normal, more, most extreme.

Example: "I was a little nervous before the presentation. Then I was very nervous. By the time I got on stage, I was sweating so much I could've solved California's drought problem."

Outliers:

- Use the "One of these things is not like the others" principle;
- Create lists where one item doesn't belong;
- Set up patterns, then break them unexpectedly.

Example: "Our company values integrity, innovation, teamwork, and casual Fridays."

Metaphors and Similes:

- Create unexpected comparisons;
- Use relatable objects or experiences in surprising ways;
- Exaggerate comparisons for comedic effect.

Example: "Trying to understand our old filing system was like trying to solve a Rubik's Cube blindfolded, underwater, while being chased by sharks."

Specificity:

- Use precise details instead of general statements;
- Name-drop specific brands, places, or people;
- The more specific and unexpected, the funnier it often is.

Example: Instead of saying, "I was tired," say, "I was so tired, I made a pot of coffee using Red Bull instead of water."

Misdirection:

- Set up an expectation, then go in a completely different direction;
- Use the element of surprise;
- Build tension, then release it unexpectedly.

Example: "After years of hard work, dedication, and sacrifice, I finally achieved my dream... of having a reasonably organized desk drawer."

Self-deprecation:

- Make yourself the butt of the joke (in moderation);
- Share relatable flaws or mistakes;
- Show humility and relatability.

Example: "I consider myself a fitness expert. I've started a new diet every Monday for the last ten years."

Remember, the key to using these strategies effectively is practice and knowing your audience. What works in one context might fall flat in another. When in doubt, a well-timed, self-deprecating joke is often the safest bet. Unless you're performing heart surgery. Then maybe just focus on the task at hand.

Pro Tip: Don't step on the laughs. If your audience is laughing, let them. You've earned it, champ.

Humor is a powerful tool, but like any power tool, it can take your finger off if you're not careful. Use it wisely, and you'll have your audience in the palm of your hand. Use it poorly, and you'll have them checking their watches and planning their escape routes.

Now go forth and find the funny. Just don't blame me if you end up with your own Netflix special. (But seriously, if you do, call me. We'll talk royalties.) Now that we've got a strong grasp on the Verbal Stage Language, let's move along the second of our Five Stage Languages.

VOCAL
IMAGE

CHAPTER 5

LUCY, ALANIS, AND THE ART OF THE VOCAL LANGUAGE

(OR HOW TO MAKE YOUR VOICE MORE ICONIC THAN A CHOCOLATE FACTORY CONVEYOR BELT MISHAP)

> *"My voice was my tool to reach people. It was more than just speaking; it was about conveying emotion, truth, and change."*
>
> **— Cicely Tyson**

THE IMAGE OF YOUR VOICE

Lucille Ball's exaggerated high-pitched "Ewwww!" reverberating through your living room. Or Alanis Morissette's breathy, emotionally charged vocals filling your headphones. Now imagine Eddie Murphy or Jim Carrey manipulating their voices to amplify their comedic timing. What do these voices have in common? They're unforgettable. They're iconic. They are powerful instruments that create indelible impressions, evoke deep emotions, and leave lasting impacts.

All voices, not just the famous ones, add meaning to the words, stories, and ideas they share. Sometimes, this happens without us even being aware of it. Your voice—yes, yours—is a signature element of who you are, just as Lucille's was to her character in *I Love Lucy*.

In the previous chapter of the book, you crafted the right words to tell your story with the first of the *Five Stage Languages*. In the next few chapters, we will explore the delivery of those words. This chapter dives deep into the art of vocal image. It doesn't matter how good your words are if people can't hear you, are distracted by unclear vocal habits, or struggle to pay attention because there isn't enough contrast in your voice. We will explore how performers like Alanis Morissette use breathy intimacy to draw listeners in, how comedians like Eddie Murphy and Jim Carrey manipulate their voices for maximum impact, and how you can harness these same techniques to make your voice a powerful tool for connection and storytelling.

As my friend D'Arcy Webb, known as "The Speech Diva" and one of the best voice educators in the world, puts it:

> "If you want people to listen to your stories, then *compel* them to listen. Egg them on. Lure them in with choice words, well-spoken choice words. Learn how to infuse your words with magic and music. It's not enough to just tell a good story. If you're speaking too quickly, if you're nasal, if you're making a picnic's worth of word sandwiches (a yummy term I've coined for jumbled or slurred speech), or if you're constantly speaking with a vocal fry, it makes it harder for the listener to absorb the story. And what happens to your story then? It gets

lost and soon forgotten, like the other tube sock you swore was with the rest of the laundry."

VOCAL MECHANICS 101: UNDERSTANDING AND MASTERING YOUR VOICE

Your voice is like a finely tuned sports car—understanding its mechanics can help you drive it to its full potential. Let's get under the hood and look at how this incredible instrument of yours actually works.

This is the breakdown:

1. Impulse and Breath: It all starts with an impulse—that urge to communicate. This impulse sends a signal to your body, kickstarting the breath that will fuel your voice.
2. Vocal Folds and Oscillations: As that breath leaves your lungs, it meets your vocal folds. These folds vibrate (or *oscillate*, if we're being fancy), creating the raw frequencies of your voice.
3. Resonators: Next, these frequencies get amplified by your body's natural resonators—your chest, throat, mouth, and nasal passages. Think of these as the speakers that give your voice its richness and depth.
4. Articulation: Finally, your lips, tongue, and teeth shape these sounds into words. Consonants happen when two articulators meet, while vowels are shaped by the movement of your lips and tongue.

Your voice isn't just a disembodied sound—it's a full-body experience. Every part of you contributes to its unique timbre, just like every part of a guitar or piano contributes to its sound. And just like those instruments, how you use and maintain your voice will affect its quality and power.

THE BREATH OF EMOTION: HOW YOUR VOICE CARRIES FEELING

Let's talk about the secret sauce that makes your voice truly powerful—emotion. Your voice isn't only a megaphone for your words; it's a direct line to your feelings, and those feelings are what truly connect you with your audience.

Think about Alanis Morissette's "You Oughta Know" or "Head Over Feet." Her breathy, intimate vocal style doesn't just convey words—it carries complex emotions like heartbreak, anger, and tenderness. It makes her music personal and relatable in a way that transcends the lyrics alone.

Or consider Celine Dion's performances. She takes us on an emotional journey, from the soft, breathy openings of "My Heart Will Go On" to those powerful, soaring notes that have become her trademark. This control over pitch, pace, and punch allows her to guide the audience's emotions, demonstrating the importance of mastering these vocal levers.

BREAKING FREE: THE IMPACT OF SOCIAL CONDITIONING ON YOUR VOICE

> *"Your voice is like a fingerprint; no two are alike, and the world needs to hear yours."*
>
> **— Kristin Chenoweth**

It is the first day of fifth grade, and I realize the teacher is calling names alphabetically by first name. I start to prepare, but I can feel the familiar dark hole of anxiety in my gut.

"Lisa?"

"Here."

"Mary?"

"Here."

"Mike?"

I hope that whatever comes out of my mouth doesn't betray me like it has at all the other schools before this one.

"Here," I say, knowing that I failed again.

At lunch, they'd all be asking me, "Are you a girl?" "Do you like boys?" And by the end of the week, I'd once again wish I sounded different. I hated my voice, and I knew that every time I opened my mouth it screamed, "Bully this future little gay kid."

For years, I didn't trust my own voice. It felt like a traitor, always ready to expose my deepest insecurities to the world. But little did I know, this struggle would become the catalyst for my journey into understanding the power of vocal expression.

It might surprise you that your voice isn't entirely your own. At least, not in the way you might think. From the moment we start making sounds, society shapes how we use our voices.

"Good girls don't yell." "Real men don't cry." Sound familiar? These messages create vocal habits that can inhibit our natural expression. Over time, our voices adapt to these constraints, often leading to a loss of authenticity.

These adaptations can cause all sorts of vocal distortions. Maybe you tighten your throat to lower your pitch, push the sound into your head to avoid expressing vulnerability, or create a nasal tone to protect against emotional exposure. These distortions become our vocal identity, often limiting our ability to communicate fully and effectively.

But here's the good news: you can reclaim your voice. Performers like Kristin Chenoweth, who uses her high-pitched voice to defy expectations, and Viola Davis, who commands attention with her resonant voice, challenge these norms. They embrace their unique vocal styles as reflections of their identity.

DIRECTOR'S CUT: THE SOUND OF OPPRESSION: RECLAIMING YOUR VOICE

Our voices can be sources of joy and self-expression, but for many, they've also been targets of criticism, bullying, and control. From childhood teasing about "funny" accents to professional settings where certain voices are deemed more "appropriate" than others, our vocal identities have often been shaped by external pressures rather than internal authenticity.

This oppression can manifest in various ways:

1. Accent discrimination: People with non-standard accents often face prejudice in social and professional settings.
2. Gender expectations: Women may be criticized for vocal fry or high-pitched voices, while men might be mocked for "feminine" tones. Vocal fry is in the lower range of your vocal register that produces a gravelly, creaky, breathy sound.
3. Cultural suppression: Individuals from minority cultures might feel pressured to alter their natural speech patterns to "fit in" with the dominant culture.

These experiences can lead to a deep-seated discomfort with our own voices, making us hesitant to speak up or express ourselves fully.

But here's the empowering truth: Your voice, with all its unique qualities, is a vital part of your identity. It carries your history, your culture, your personality. By embracing and cultivating your authentic voice, you're not just improving your communication skills—you're reclaiming a fundamental part of yourself.

As you work through the exercises in this book, remember that the goal isn't to erase your vocal quirks or to sound like someone else. It is to amplify your true voice, to let it ring out clear and strong, free from the constraints of past criticism or societal expectations.

Your voice is your power. Take it back.

VOICES FROM EVERY STAGE: FROM TED TALKS TO EVERYDAY HEROES

While we can learn a lot from the Lucille Balls and Alanis Morissettes of the world, the power of voice isn't reserved for the famous. Let's zoom in on some examples that might hit closer to home.

Consider the world of TED and TEDx talks. These platforms have given voice to countless individuals, each with their unique vocal signature. Take Brené Brown's 2010 TEDx Houston talk on vulnerability. Her warm, conversational tone and strategic use of pauses helped turn a potentially uncomfortable topic into a viral sensation with over fifty million views. Brown's voice conveyed authenticity and vulnerability, perfectly matching her message.

Or think about Sir Ken Robinson's legendary TED Talk, "Do Schools Kill Creativity?" His dry British humor, perfectly timed pauses, and varied pacing kept the audience engaged while delivering a powerful message about education reform. Robinson's voice became a tool for both entertainment and persuasion.

Let's bring it even closer to home. I have had the privilege of working with countless individuals who've transformed their vocal presence. Take Chris, a tech executive. He started out speaking in a monotone, rushing through hispresentations as if he couldn't wait to be off stage. Through our work together, Chris learned to vary his pitch and pace, to use strategic pauses, and to infuse hisvoice with the passion he felt for her work. The result? His team presentations went from forgettable to inspiring, and he soon found herself invited to speak at industry conferences.

Then there's Charles, a non-profit leader who came to me speaking so softly that his important message literally got lost. We worked on his breath support and vocal projection, not to make him louder, but to give his voice the strength to match his convictions. Now, when Marcus speaks about his organization's mission, his voice carries not just volume, but authority and passion that inspire action.

These examples—from globally recognized TED speakers to professionals similar to you or your colleagues—demonstrate that vocal mastery isn't about having a "perfect" voice. It means learning to use your unique voice effectively to connect, persuade, and inspire.

As we dive into the Five Vocal Levers in the next section, keep these diverse examples in mind. Whether you're aiming for a TED stage, leading a team meeting, or simply wanting to express yourself more authentically in your daily life, these tools can help you harness the full power of your voice.

Every voice has the potential to make an impact. Yours included. Let's discover how to unlock that potential.

THE FIVE VOCAL LEVERS: FROM IMPROV TO IMPACT

Let me take you back to where this all began for me—the wild, unpredictable world of improv theater.

You're on stage, the lights are hot, and you have no script. The audience shouts out a random location and character, and suddenly, you're a pirate captain on the moon. How do you make that believable? How do you get your fellow improvisers to understand and build on your idea? How do you make the audience feel the gravity (or lack thereof) of the situation?

The answer, my friends, is in your voice.

In improv, we had to become vocal chameleons, able to change our vocal delivery at the drop of a hat. We needed to generate ideas, evoke emotions, change the energy of a scene, and clarify our intentions for both our scene partners and the audience—all without the luxury of rehearsal or scripted lines.

It was in the pressure cooker of those improv performances that I began to recognize patterns in how we used our voices to achieve different effects. Whether it was lowering our pitch to convey authority, speeding up our pace to create urgency, or using strategic pauses to build suspense, we were intuitively using what I would later codify as the Five Vocal Levers.

These levers—Pitch, Pace, Punch, Pause, and Passion—became the backbone of my approach to vocal mastery. They are not just theoretical concepts; they are practical tools born from the need to communicate effectively in high-pressure, high-stakes situations.

As I transitioned from improv stages to corporate boardrooms and TED talks, I realized that the same techniques that helped create believable pirate captains on the moon could help CEOs deliver compelling presentations, thought leaders inspire audiences, and everyday people communicate with more confidence and impact.

As we explore each of these levers, I invite you to think of yourself as an improv artist. Your life is the stage, every conversation is a new scene, and your voice is your most versatile prop. Let's learn how to use it to its fullest potential.

THE FIVE VOCAL LEVERS: MASTERING YOUR VOCAL TOOLBOX

> *"You are perfectly cast in your life. I can't imagine anyone but you in the role. Go play."*
>
> **— Lin-Manuel Miranda**

See that 800 lb gorilla? Let's deal with it: why do we hate listening to our own voices so much? If you're like most of my clients, the thought of hearing your recorded voice probably makes you cringe harder than my toddler when I suggest brushing her teeth.

Our voices are for other people.

The voice you hear in your head is different from what others hear. It conducts itself through your bones and open spaces, making it sound deeper and more resonant. Plus, you're used to hearing your voice from behind itself—your ears are behind your mouth, after all. When you hear a recording, it strips away this internal resonance, revealing a sound that feels foreign.

But remember this: your voice is perfect as it is. Your vocal instrument is finely tuned by your life experiences and emotional landscape, ready to convey your story profoundly and authentically. And with these five levers, you'll learn to play it like a virtuoso.

Pitch: The Emotional Scale

Pitch is the foundation of vocal expression. It is not just about being high or low—it's about how the height of your voice influences the emotional content of your speech.

Take Viola Davis, for example. Her deep, resonant voice commands attention and conveys gravitas. Watch her 2015 Emmy acceptance speech, and you'll see how she uses pitch to draw the audience into her message, starting low to establish authority, then raising her pitch to emphasize passion.

On the flip side, we have Kristin Chenoweth. Her high-pitched, playful voice might seem like the opposite of powerful, but she uses it to create charm and accessibility. Just listen to her performance of "Popular" in *Wicked*—a masterclass in using a lighter tone to captivate an audience.

In my years of coaching, I've seen pitch work wonders in unexpected ways. I once worked with a tech CEO who spoke in a perpetually high, anxious pitch that undermined her authority. We worked on lowering her pitch for key moments, and the change was dramatic. Not only did her team respond more positively, but she reported feeling more confident and in control.

Pitch isn't about mimicking someone else's voice. Find the full range of your own voice and learn when to deploy different parts of that range for maximum impact.

Action:

Choose a sentence and deliver it first in a low pitch, then in a high pitch. Notice how the emotional impact changes. For example, say, "This is important," in a deep voice to convey seriousness, then repeat it in a higher pitch to express urgency.

Pace: The Rhythm of Storytelling

Pace is all about the speed at which you speak. It is like the heartbeat of your story—too fast, and it becomes overwhelming; too slow, and it loses momentum.

Consider Beyoncé's song "Formation." She uses rapid verses to build energy and momentum, contrasting with slower, more deliberate passages that draw the listener in and emphasize emotion. It is a perfect example of pacing that creates a dynamic performance and keeps the audience engaged.

Or think about Jim Carrey in *Liar Liar*. He switches between fast, manic pacing to convey chaos or excitement and slower pacing to build up to a punchline or surprising twist. His timing showcases how both comedy and drama can be enhanced when you manipulate pace.

Pace was a game-changer in my improv days. We'd use rapid-fire delivery to build energy in a scene, then suddenly slow down to highlight a crucial moment. This contrast kept the audience on the edge of their seats.

I have brought this technique into my coaching. I worked with a non-profit leader who tended to rush through his organization's mission statement, diminishing its impact. We practiced slowing down on key phrases, allowing each word to land. The result? His passion shone through, and donations increased at his next fundraiser.

Action:

> Take a short speech or passage and mark where you will intentionally speed up or slow down. Practice delivering it with these intentional shifts to see how this changes the emotional tone of the delivery.

Punch (Volume and Intensity): The Power of Impact

Punch is not just being loud or soft—it's about using volume strategically to emphasize points, create contrast, and convey emotion.

Celine Dion is a master of volume control. Listen to "My Heart Will Go On" and you'll hear her move effortlessly from soft, delicate whispers to powerful, resonant belts. She uses volume to create an emotional journey, guiding the listener through crescendos of intensity and valleys of introspection.

Nor is punch just about being loud—it's about strategic emphasis. I learned this lesson the hard way during an improv show when I tried to steal a scene by simply shouting my lines. It didn't work. The audience was put off, and my fellow performers were thrown off balance.

This experience informs how I coach *punch* today. I guide clients to use volume spikes selectively, saving them for moments of true importance. I once worked with a soft-spoken author who was struggling to engage audiences at book readings. We identified key passages where a volume boost could heighten emotional impact. The change was remarkable. Suddenly, her readings were dynamic events that left audiences spellbound.

Action:

Choose a line and deliver it in three ways: whispering, speaking softly, and projecting loudly. Notice how the volume changes the meaning or impact of the words. For example, say, "I can't believe it," softly to express disbelief, then loudly to convey shock or anger.

Pause: The Power of Silence

Never underestimate the power of a well-placed pause. A moment of silence can be as impactful as any spoken word.

Think about Oprah Winfrey's Golden Globe acceptance speech. Her deliberate pauses after emotional or powerful moments allowed the audience to absorb her message of justice and truth, adding depth to her words.

Or consider Barack Obama, a master of the strategic pause. In speeches like his 2008 victory address, he paused after key phrases, creating anticipation and allowing his points about unity and hope to resonate with the audience.

In improv, we have a saying: "If you're lost, pause." It is counterintuitive—when you're uncertain, the impulse is often to fill the silence. But a well-placed pause can give you time to think, build suspense, and often prompt your scene partner to jump in with a great idea.

This principle translates beautifully to public speaking. I worked with a TED speaker who was rushing through her talk, afraid that pauses would lose the audience's attention. We practiced strategic pausing, especially after key points or rhetorical questions. The impact was immediate: her ideas had room to breathe, and audience engagement skyrocketed. Her TEDx has over 2 million views on YouTube.

Action:

Read a short speech or passage and mark where you could add a pause for effect. Practice delivering it with these pauses, paying attention to how the silence changes the flow and impact of the speech.

DIRECTOR'S CUT: HUMOR AND THE VOICE: THE SOUND OF LAUGHTER

We have explored how pace and pauses contribute to humor; let's dive deeper into how your voice can tickle funny bones.

Pacing: Comedy is all about timing. A well-timed acceleration or deceleration can heighten the comedic effect. Think of how stand-up comedians rush through a set-up and then slow down for the punchline.

Pausing: The "pregnant pause" is a comedian's best friend. It builds anticipation and gives the audience time to catch up, making the punchline even more impactful.

Pitch: Varying your pitch can add layers to your humor. A sudden shift from low to high pitch can underscore the absurdity of a situation, while a gradual pitch change can build comedic tension.

Volume: Strategic volume changes can emphasize the humor in your words. A whispered aside or a sudden loud exclamation can catch your audience off guard, amplifying the comedic effect.

Remember, humor is about surprise, and your voice is the perfect tool to create that surprise. Play with these elements, and you might just find your inner comic voice!

Passion: The Emotional Core of Your Voice

"Speech isn't just about speaking correctly, or sounding mellifluous, or like you have gravitas. It's about meaning what you say. And saying it with a full heart."

– D'Arcy Webb (my dear friend and voice coach extraordinaire)

Passion is the emotional energy that infuses your voice. It conveys how much you care about what you're saying through your vocal emphasis, tone, and the intensity of your delivery.

Listen to Alanis Morissette's "You Oughta Know." Her voice is infused with raw emotion, making the listener feel every word deeply. Her vocal delivery makes the music profoundly personal and relatable. She balances an overly breathy delivery with a change in her vocal register to bring us to the deeper parts of her range.

Passion turns a good performance into an unforgettable one. In improv, we called it "heightening the scene" —finding the emotional core of a scene and amplifying it.

I see the same principle at work in all forms of communication. I once coached a brilliant climate scientist whose presentations were dry and technical. We worked on connecting her to the passion that drove her research. When she allowed that passion to infuse her voice, her presentations transformed from data dumps to inspiring calls to action.

Passion doesn't mean manufacturing emotion—allow your genuine enthusiasm and conviction to shine through in your voice.

Action:

> Take a sentence and practice emphasizing different words to change the emotional impact. For instance, "I need you to listen," can be delivered with an emphasis on "need" to show urgency or on "listen" to convey the importance of the action.

Bringing It All Together

These five levers—Pitch, Pace, Punch, Pause, and Passion—are your toolkit for vocal mastery. But like any tool, their power lies in how you use them. The key is practice and mindful application.

In my workshops, we spend time experimenting with each lever individually, then combine them for maximum impact. Like learning to play an instrument, first you master individual notes, then chords, and finally full songs.

As you continue through this book, I encourage you to play with these levers in your daily communications. Pay attention to how you naturally use them and experiment with pushing your boundaries. You might be surprised at the untapped potential in your voice.

Your voice is unique. These levers don't mean changing who you are—they help you become the fullest, most impactful version of yourself. So let's raise the curtain on your vocal performance.

THE EMOTIONAL LANGUAGE OF VOWELS AND CONSONANTS

Vowels are where much of the emotion in your speech lives. Think about how Oprah stretches her vowels to convey excitement or joy. Vowels are the breath of your voice, allowing you to express the depth of your feelings. How you shape these vowels with your lips and tongue can significantly alter the emotional impact of your message.

They are the sustained sounds that carry the melody of your speech. When you elongate a vowel, you give your audience more time to feel the emotion behind your words. Think about how a passionate speaker might say, "It's amaaaazing!" The extended "*a*" sound lets that excitement resonate with the listener.

But don't forget about consonants! While vowels carry emotion, consonants provide structure. The skeletal frame of your spoken word. They are formed when two articulators meet—like your lips, teeth, or tongue—giving your words clarity and form. (Fun fact: When my daughter was learning to speak, we practiced forming the "P" in "Papi" by pressing our lips together and the "V" in her name, "Viviana," by bringing our bottom lip to our top teeth.)

In my workshops, I often use this exercise: Take a simple phrase like, "I love you," and play with the vowels and consonants. Draw out the "*o*" in *love* for warmth and affection. Sharpen the "*v*" for intensity. By adjusting these elements, you'll find that the same three words can convey a whole spectrum of emotions.

PROTECTING YOUR VOICE: HOW WE LOSE OUR WAY

"Being oppressed means the absence of choices."

— bell hooks

Our voices often lose their natural expression due to societal conditioning and self-protection mechanisms. From a young age, we're taught to control our voices. "Good girls don't yell," and, "Real men don't cry." These messages create vocal habits that inhibit our natural expression.

Over time, our voices adapt to these constraints, leading to what I call "voice distortions." You might tighten your throat to lower your pitch, push the sound into your head to avoid expressing vulnerability, or create a nasal tone to protect against emotional exposure. These distortions become our vocal identity, often limiting our ability to communicate fully and effectively.

I have seen this play out countless times. I once worked with a female tech entrepreneur who had adopted a clipped, low-pitched speaking style in an attempt to be taken more seriously in her male-dominated field. The result? She sounded inauthentic and strained. We worked on reclaiming her natural voice, incorporating its natural warmth and variety. Not only did she feel more comfortable, but her speeches became more compelling and authentic.

EMBRACING YOUR VOCAL IDENTITY

> *"A lot of people are afraid to say what they want. That's why they don't get what they want."*
>
> **– Madonna**

Madonna hits the nail on the head. Your voice is more than just the way you sound—it's a powerful communication tool that gives voice to your dreams, experiences, and desires. Embracing your true vocal identity is about having the courage to let your authentic self shine through in your voice.

Your voice is uniquely yours. It is an instrument finely tuned by your life experiences and emotional landscape. The goal isn't to sound like someone else—it's to be the most authentic, powerful version of yourself.

In my workshops, I often use this exercise to help people reconnect with their authentic voice:

> Close your eyes and think of a time when you felt completely free to express yourself. Maybe it was laughing with close friends, or in a heated debate about something you're passionate about. Remember how your voice felt in that moment: its tone, its rhythm, its energy. That is your authentic voice. That is the voice we want to nurture and strengthen.

As we move forward, I challenge you to pay attention to moments when you feel your voice shift away from that authentic place. What triggered the change? How can you bring yourself back to your true voice? I encourage you to spend the next two weeks choosing a different thing to focus on each day in your normal interactions and then look back and consider how that's helped your become more aware of the choices you make. For example, "On Monday, I focus on making strategic pauses. On Tuesday, I focus on my pacing."

Your voice has the power to move people, to inspire change, to connect deeply with others. But that power comes from embracing your unique vocal identity, not from trying to fit into someone else's mold.

So, let's raise our voices—in all their unique, authentic, powerful glory. Before we move on to the third of the Five Stage Languages (The Physical Language), I want to give you some more Vocal Language support by exploring a few of the Vocal Archetypes I see often in my coaching work.

** Don't forget to check out:
www.mikeganino.com/bookresources
to grab a free vocal warmup training to keep your pipes piping. **

DIRECTOR'S CUT

Speaking of authenticity, we need to address an important point when it comes to vocal expression. We need to talk about mimicking voices. I get it—you want to make your story more vivid, more engaging. But here's the deal: if your story doesn't work in your own voice, or that of your people of origin, it might be time to rethink your approach.

Let me be blunt: imitating accents from another culture or race? It rarely lands well and often offends. Trust me, I've seen it backfire more times than I can count. And don't even get me started on cis straight folks putting on a stereotypical "gay" male voice to make a point. Just. Don't.

The same goes for using African-American Vernacular English (AAVE) if it's not your natural way of speaking. It is not a costume you can put on and take off for effect.

You might be thinking, "But what if I am of the same race, orientation, or gender expression?" Even then, pause and ask yourself: Is this vocal impression really necessary to make your point? Or are you just reinforcing negative stereotypes?

Your authentic voice is powerful enough. You don't need to borrow someone else's to make an impact. Focus on telling your stories in ways that uplift and unite, not divide and offend.

Make a scene, absolutely. But make it with your *own* voice.

CHAPTER 5.5

VOCAL ARCHETYPES: THE NINE VOICES OF IMPACTFUL COMMUNICATION

"The human voice is the most perfect instrument of all."

– Ariana DeBose

In my years of coaching, I've noticed that great communicators have a remarkable ability to adapt their vocal style to different situations. It is like they have access to a wardrobe of voices, each perfectly suited for a specific purpose. I call these styles "Vocal Archetypes." Understanding and mastering these archetypes can dramatically enhance your communication effectiveness. Consider this a bit of an advanced Masterclass in voice work that can help you as you continue to expand the choices you can make vocally. Let's explore each of the nine archetypes:

The Motivator

This is the voice of inspiration, the one that rallies troops and ignites passion. It is the sound of possibility and encouragement.

Key characteristics:

- Passion poured into every vowel;
- Increased rate of speech;
- Legato (smooth and connected) delivery;
- High energy;
- Varied pitch for emphasis.

I once worked with a startup founder who struggled to inspire her team during tough times. We tapped into her inner Motivator, and suddenly her team meetings went from dull status updates to energizing strategy sessions. The key was learning to infuse her words with genuine passion and energy.

The Motivator voice is particularly effective when you need to boost morale, drive action, or inspire change. It is the voice of coaches in locker rooms, leaders during crises, and speakers at motivational events.

Action:

Think of a goal you're passionate about. Now, speak about it using the Motivator voice. Increase your energy, speed up your pace, and let your passion shine through every word. Notice how it feels different from your usual speaking style.

The Educator

This is the voice of knowledge and insight. It is clear, structured, and focused on imparting understanding.

Key characteristics:

- Slower rate of speech;
- More frequent pauses;
- Matter-of-fact pitch;
- Clear articulation;
- Emphasis on key points.

One of my clients, a brilliant scientist, had groundbreaking research but struggled to communicate it effectively. By embracing the Educator archetype, she learned to pace her delivery and use strategic pauses, allowing her audience to absorb her complex ideas.

The Educator voice is invaluable when explaining complex concepts, teaching new skills, or sharing important information. It is the voice of professors in lecture halls, experts on panels, and anyone in a teaching role.

Action:

Explain a concept you know well (it could be a hobby or a work process) using the Educator voice. Slow down your speech, use clear articulation, and incorporate pauses after key points. Notice how this style helps to clarify and structure your explanation.

The Coach

This voice guides and instructs. It is direct, clear, and action-oriented, pushing others towards growth and achievement.

Key characteristics:

- Increased volume (punch);
- Staccato (short, detached notes) delivery;
- Direct and punchy tone;
- Consistent pace and rhythm;
- Clear, concise instructions.

I have used this archetype myself when working with clients who need a push. The Coach voice helps cut through hesitation and drives action. It is particularly effective when you need to give feedback, provide clear direction, or motivate someone to push past their perceived limits.

The Coach voice is the sound of personal trainers in the gym, life coaches pushing for breakthroughs, and managers providing constructive feedback.

Action:

Think of a piece of advice you'd like to give someone. Deliver it using the Coach voice. Be direct, use a punchy tone, and focus on clear, actionable instructions. Feel the difference in the impact of your words.

The Friend

This is the voice of connection and relatability. It is casual, warm, and inviting, creating a sense of trust and openness.

Key characteristics:

- Conversational tone;
- Melodic variation;
- Casual pacing;
- Natural rhythm;
- Open, warm tone.

I often advise corporate leaders to adopt elements of the Friend archetype when they want to build trust and rapport with their teams. It is amazing how a shift to a more conversational tone can transform the dynamic of a meeting.

The Friend voice is perfect for building relationships, having difficult conversations, or creating a comfortable atmosphere. It is the voice of close confidants, empathetic listeners, and anyone looking to establish a genuine connection.

Action:

Share a personal story using the Friend voice. Keep your tone conversational, let your speech have a natural rhythm, and allow for melodic variation. Notice how this style can make even a prepared story feel spontaneous and relatable.

The Caretaker

This voice nurtures and comforts. It is gentle, supportive, and focused on creating a sense of safety and well-being.

Key characteristics:

- Softer pitch;
- Calming pace;
- Lower volume;
- Gentle tone;
- Soothing rhythm.

I have seen the power of the Caretaker voice in crisis communication scenarios. Leaders who can access this archetype in tough times often build deeper, more lasting connections with their teams.

The Caretaker voice is essential when dealing with sensitive issues, providing emotional support, or creating a sense of security. It is the voice of counselors in therapy sessions, nurses with patients, and anyone in a nurturing role.

Action:

Think of a comforting message you'd like to convey. Deliver it using the Caretaker voice. Soften your pitch, lower your volume, and maintain a calm, soothing pace. Feel how this vocal style can create a sense of safety and comfort.

The Authority

This is the voice of command and expertise. It is the tone that makes people sit up and listen, conveying confidence and credibility.

Key characteristics:

- Lower pitch;
- Measured pace;
- Clear enunciation;
- Minimal vocal variation;
- Steady volume.

I once worked with a young executive struggling to be taken seriously in board meetings. By adopting elements of the Authority archetype—lowering her pitch slightly, slowing her pace, and minimizing unnecessary vocal fluctuations—she was able to command the room's attention and respect.

The Authority voice isn't about intimidation; it instills confidence. It is particularly useful when you need to establish credibility quickly, make important announcements, or lead in high-stakes situations.

Action:

Take a simple statement and deliver it as if you're the ultimate authority on the subject. Lower your pitch, slow your pace, and keep your volume steady. Notice how this changes the impact of your words.

The Storyteller

This voice captivates and engages. It is the voice that can turn even the most mundane information into a fascinating tale.

Key characteristics:

- Dynamic pitch range;
- Varied pacing;
- Use of dramatic pauses;
- Expressive tone;
- Vivid vocal coloring.

One of my favorite success stories involves a data analyst who needed to present complex findings to non-technical stakeholders. By tapping into the Storyteller archetype, he transformed dry statistics into a compelling narrative. His presentations went from being a necessary evil to a highly anticipated event.

The Storyteller voice is invaluable when you need to make information memorable or want to create an emotional connection with your audience. It is the voice of charismatic public speakers, engaging podcast hosts, and anyone who needs to capture and hold attention.

Action:

Take a simple event from your day and turn it into a short story. Use varied pacing, incorporate dramatic pauses, and let your voice be expressive. See how this can turn even an ordinary anecdote into an engaging tale.

The Innovator

This voice crackles with possibility and potential. It is the sound of the future, new ideas, and exciting changes.

Key characteristics:

- Enthusiastic tone;
- Quick pace with strategic pauses;
- Forward-leaning energy;
- Slightly higher pitch;
- Dynamic volume changes.

I have used this archetype myself when introducing new coaching techniques to skeptical clients. The Innovator voice helps to generate excitement and openness to new ideas.

This voice is particularly effective when you're introducing change, pitching new ideas, or trying to inspire creative thinking in others. It is the voice of tech entrepreneurs unveiling new products, thought leaders introducing novel concepts, and change agents in any field.

Action:

Think of a new idea or a change you'd like to propose. Present it using the Innovator voice. Speak with enthusiasm, use a quicker pace with strategic pauses, and let your excitement come through in your tone. Feel how this energizes your proposal.

The Analyst

This voice prioritizes clarity and precision. It is the voice of logic and data-driven insights.

Key characteristics:

- Precise articulation;
- Measured pace;
- Minimal emotional inflection;
- Emphasis on key data points;
- Consistent volume.

I once coached a passionate non-profit leader struggling to secure funding. Her heart-driven appeals weren't landing with data-focused donors. By incorporating the Analyst archetype, she learned to present her organization's impact with clarity and precision, significantly improving her fundraising success.

The Analyst voice is crucial when you need to convey complex information, present data, or make logical arguments. It is the voice of financial advisors explaining market trends, researchers discussing study findings, and anyone needing to communicate detailed, factual information.

Action:

Take a set of facts or figures and present them using the Analyst voice. Focus on precise articulation, maintain a measured pace, and emphasize key data points. Notice how this style makes complex information more digestible and impactful.

The power of these archetypes lies not in rigidly adhering to one, but in your ability to flow between them as the situation demands. Great communicators are vocal chameleons, able to adapt their voice to best serve their message and their audience.

As you move forward, challenge yourself to identify these archetypes in the speakers around you. More importantly, experiment with them in your own communication. You might be surprised at how expanding your vocal range can enhance your ability to connect, influence, and lead in all areas of your life. Now that we've explored the Verbal and Vocal Languages, it's time to move on to our third of the Five Stage Languages: The Physical Language.

GESTURES
LET YOUR
Body
TALK!
EXPRESSIONS
POSTURE
GROUNDING

CHAPTER 6

THE BODY SPEAKS: HARNESSING PHYSICAL ENERGY IN STORYTELLING

(OR HOW TO GESTICULATE WITHOUT LOOKING LIKE YOU'RE SWATTING INVISIBLE FLIES)

"The body never lies."

– Rita Moreno

THE TRUTH IN OUR BODIES

She pulls my hands tighter around her belly. I hear the sweet little whisper of a four-year-old: "It's gonna be a big surprise, Papi." And as the log we are sitting on reaches the top of the treadmill-like track that lifts it to the top of the chute—we see the flash of sunlight, and then the big surprise.

A forty-two-foot free fall into a pool of water that promises to soak us.

Right before the log drops, I feel her diaphragm tense up. Her body is responding to the big surprise—to the moment of fear.

We've done this plenty of times, and she begs every morning to go to Knott's Berry Farm (an amusement park in Southern California) in order to ride the "log ride." She knows she is safe, and she looks forward to it.

And yet my daughter's little belly tightens, her breath catches for a minute, and she responds to what's in front of her.

So do we.

Every time we stand in front of an audience about to communicate something, our body responds and we send signals, messages, and frequencies out to the audience from that physical state.

This is all about energy creation: as we move, as we walk, as we shift our physicality, we create energy. And let me tell you, that energy is more contagious than a yawn in a sleepy classroom.

Our bodies are like those mood rings we all had as kids (come on, admit it, you had one too). They constantly change colors, revealing our true emotions even when we try to play it cool. The problem is, most of us have been taught to fear that energy, to bottle it up like we're storing lightning in a jar. Spoiler alert: it doesn't work, and you might just end up with crispy eyebrows.

We're meant to experience the world through our bodies. And yet, our society straps us into bondage that limits the range of our expression – don't be too angry, too emotional, too loud, too happy -- from our first breath. Sometimes, even before. It is like we're all starring in our own personal straitjacket fashion show. Not a great look, folks.

You have the right words, and you deliver them with an amazing voice, but if you are standing like a petrified tree on the stage, you are diminishing the impact that you could have. In this chapter, you'll break free from that invisible strait-jacket. You will learn how to harness that physical energy, to let it flow through you and into your stories. Because when you do, magic happens. And who doesn't want a little magic in their presentations?

THE POWER OF INTENTIONAL MOVEMENT

Let's talk about what happens when we ignore our bodies or, worse, when we let bad habits take over. It is like watching a car crash in slow motion, except the car is your presentation, and the crash is your audience's attention span going splat.

You're giving the presentation of your life. Your slides are on point, your data is rock solid, and you've practiced your speech more times than you've watched your favorite Netflix series (impressive, I know). But as soon as you step on stage, it's like your body goes rogue.

Either you freeze in one spot like you've just seen Medusa in the front row, or you pace back and forth like a caged tiger with a particularly full bladder. Maybe you make random trips to visit people on either side of the stage as if you're hosting the world's most awkward cocktail party. Or perhaps you've become one with the podium, clinging to it like it's the last lifeboat on the *Titanic*.

And let's not forget the classic "ground gazer" —you know, when you walk around staring at the floor as if the answers to life, the universe, and everything are written on your shoelaces. (They're not. I checked.)

All these habits are like kryptonite to your story's superpowers. They drain away your story power faster than a toddler sharing cookies at daycare.

Aim instead for what I like to call "fully alive physicality," which is about expanding your range so that you move with purpose. Think of it like this: You are not just a speaker; you're the director of your own one-person show. And as the director, your job is to control what's in the audience's frame, because that dictates their takeaway.

So, how do you do this? How do you go from flailing fish to graceful dolphin? (Yes, I just compared you to a dolphin. Take the compliment and run with it – everyone loves dolphins.)

It starts with awareness. Next time you practice your presentation, try this:

1. Record yourself. Yes, I know, watching yourself on video is about as comfortable as a dentist appointment. Do it anyway. And yes—this is the same activity from the opening of this book. Turns out recording yourself and watching "the tape" (as they say in Hollywood and the NFL) is a great way to improve and bring more awareness to your choices.
2. Watch the recording with the sound off. What story is your body telling?
3. Now listen to the recording without watching. Does your voice match the energy your body gave off?

If you're like most people, you'll notice some... let's call them "creative differences" between your body and your voice. Your goal is to get them in sync, like the world's most coordinated duet.

Remember, your physical energy is a tool, just like your voice or your words. Used intentionally, it can amplify your message, draw your audience in, and make your story unforgettable. Used unintentionally... let's just say it can turn your carefully crafted presentation into an interpretive dance gone wrong.

In the next section, you'll discover how to use that physical energy to direct your audience's attention. Because let's face it, if you can't get them to look at you, they certainly won't listen to you. Unless you're invisible—in which case, we have bigger problems to discuss.

DIRECTING THE AUDIENCE'S ATTENTION: YOU'RE THE CAPTAIN NOW (SORT OF)

Here is a fun fact for you: audiences listen with their eyes. No, they haven't developed ear-balls (thank goodness, because that would be creepy). What I mean is, they're constantly watching you, reading your body language like it's the latest bestseller. And let me tell you, it can be a page-turner if you tap into it.

Your movement on stage isn't about looking good (though that's a nice bonus), but about directing attention and feelings. You are the traffic cop of emotions, using your body to tell the audience where to look and how to feel. No whistle required (unless that's part of your act, in which case, blow away).

Think of it this way: you're not just a speaker, you're a magician. And like any good magician, your job is to control where your audience looks. The difference is, instead of misdirection, you use "thisdirection." (Get it? *This* direction? I'll be here all week, folks.)

But here's the million-dollar question: are you using this superpower intentionally, or are you accidentally hypnotizing your audience into a coma?

Let's break it down with a little game I like to call "Spot the Difference":

> **Scenario A:** You have reached a crucial point in your presentation. You stand still, make eye contact with different sections of the audience, and use a deliberate hand gesture to emphasize your words.
>
> **Scenario B:** You are making the same point, but you pace back and forth like a nervous penguin, your hands flap around like you're trying to take flight, and your eyes dart around the room like you've spotted a ghost who had too much Halloween candy and is bouncing off the ballroom walls.

Which do you think keeps your audience hanging on your every word? (Hint: It is not the one where you look like you're auditioning for a role in *Paranormal Activity: The Conference Keynote.*)

The key is intentionality. Every move you make should have a purpose. You are the director of this show, remember? So start directing!

Here is a little exercise to help you practice:

1. Take a simple message—let's say, "This new product will revolutionize the industry."
2. Now, think of three emotions you might want to convey with this message: excitement, determination, and confidence.
3. Practice delivering the message three times, each time focusing on one of those emotions. How does your body move differently for each one?
4. Bonus round: Try delivering the message while conveying the opposite emotion (like boredom). Feel weird? Good! That is your body telling you it's out of sync with your words.

Your goal is to make your physical movement support and enhance your message, not distract from it—unless your message is, "I'm nervous and I have no idea what I'm doing." In which case, by all means, keep fidgeting.

THE LANGUAGE OF THE BODY: SPEAKING WITHOUT WORDS

Pop quiz time: What's the difference between a statue and a captivating speaker?

Give up? Movement, my friends. Glorious, intentional, story-enhancing movement.

Your body has its own language, and it's time you became fluent. No Rosetta Stone required (though if someone wants to make "Body Language Rosetta Stone," I call dibs on that million-dollar idea).

Let's break down the elements of this unspoken language:

Gestures: These are the words in your body's vocabulary. They come in a few flavors:

- Illustrators: The show-offs of the gesture world. They illustrate what you say. Talking about growth? Sweep your hand upward. Describing something tiny? Pinch your fingers together. Just try not to look like you're conducting an invisible orchestra.
- Regulators: The traffic cops of conversation. Nodding, leaning in, raising a hand slightly: these all help regulate the flow of communication. Master these, and you'll never have to yell, "Hey, it's my turn to talk!" again.
- Emblems: The universally understood gestures. A thumbs up, a peace sign, a shrug. Use these wisely—a misplaced emblem can turn your serious point into an unintentional joke.

Facial Expressions: Your face is a billboard for your emotions. A raised eyebrow here, a wrinkled nose there: it all adds up to a story. Just be careful not to let your face betray you. Nothing ruins a, "We're definitely not in trouble," speech quite like looking like you just saw your stock portfolio tank.

Posture: This is the foundation of your physical presence. Good posture says, "I'm confident and engaged." Bad posture says, "I'd rather be napping." Unless you're giving a presentation on the importance of sleep, aim for the former.

Grounding: This is all about your connection to the floor. No, not literally (please don't lie down mid-presentation). Grounding means feeling stable and centered. It is the difference between looking like you're about to be blown away by a strong breeze and looking like you could weather a hurricane.

The trick is to make all these elements work together harmoniously. It is like conducting an orchestra, but instead of instruments, you're coordinating body parts. When you get it right, it's music to your audience's eyes. (See what I did there?)

Here is a quick exercise to put it all together:

1. Think of a simple story—let's say, finding a $20 bill on the street.
2. Tell the story once using only your words.
3. Now, tell it again, this time consciously using gestures, facial expressions, and posture to enhance the story.
4. Finally, tell it one more time, but intentionally make your body language contradict your words.

Feel the difference? That is the power of body language, folks. Use it wisely, and you'll have your audience in the palm of your hand. Use it poorly, and... well, at least you'll give them something to talk about at the water cooler.

Remember, your body is always speaking. The question is, are you in control of the conversation?

SPACE AND PROXIMITY: THE DANCE OF DISTANCE

Let's talk about something that sounds fancy but is super intuitive: proxemics. It's just a scholarly way of saying "how we use space." Think about the last time you were at a party - you probably moved closer to people you wanted to connect with and drifted away from the guy telling the endless fishing story. That same principle works on stage.

Most speakers fall into one of two traps: they either pace back and forth like a hyperactive squirrel on espresso, or they find one "safe" spot and become a human statue. But the stage is your dance floor, and your presentation is your chance to do the cha-cha with your audience's attention.

Picture your stage like a chessboard. Each position has its own superpower:

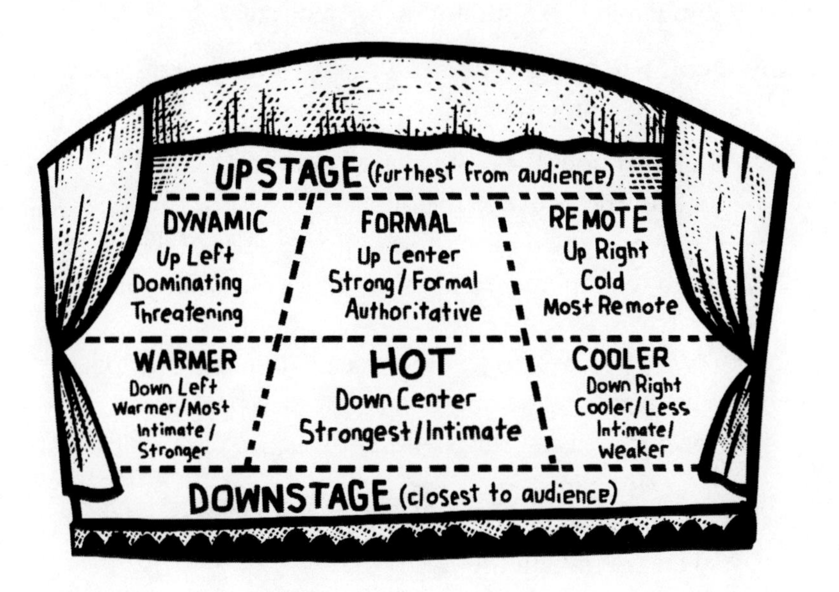

Upstage (the back):

- Center: This is your power spot. Use it when you're dropping knowledge or making bold statements. Think Obama at the inauguration.
- The corners: These are your mystery zones. Great for building tension or setting up a reveal. Like when a comedian steps back before delivering their biggest punchline.

Downstage (close to the audience):

- Center: This is your connection central. When you want to have a heart-to-heart with your audience, this is your spot. Just don't get so close that your audience can count your nostril hairs—that's a different kind of connection entirely.
- The sides: Perfect for storytelling or creating a more casual vibe. It's like sitting at the end of a bar - close enough to chat, but not in anyone's face.

Now, here's where it gets fun. You can use movement to physically illustrate your content:

- Talking about the past? Step to one side.
- The future? Move to the other.
- Comparing two ideas? Use opposite sides of the stage.
- Need to emphasize a point? Step forward like you're sharing a secret.
- Have a process, concept, or idea with more than one step, part, or section? Talk about each part from specific areas on stage so your audience builds a mental map with you.
- Want to give them space to process? Back up (just not so far you fall off the stage).

Want to test this out? Try this quick exercise:

1. Pick a simple topic, like describing your morning routine.
2. Map out your space—decide where "home" is, where "work" is, where different parts of your routine happen.
3. Now tell your story, moving to each "location" as you describe it.
4. Bonus round: Try telling the same story without moving. Feel the difference? That's the power of space, baby!

The best part? You don't need to memorize a complicated choreography. Just remember: big ideas need space; intimate moments need proximity. Move with intention, and your audience will follow your emotional journey without even realizing why.

DIRECTOR'S CUT: THE FIRST 30 SECONDS - STOP GIVING AWAY YOUR POWER!

Let's have a come-to-Jesus moment about stage entrances. Every time I see a speaker shuffle onto stage, do the awkward podium dance, or start their speech with that nervous little weight shift that looks like a bad version of the cha-cha, I want to leap from my seat and yell "CUT!"

Why? Because you're literally walking away from your power.

Think about this: The moment you step on stage, you have something magical—something most speakers desperately try to build over their entire presentation. You have:

- Every eye in the room on you
- Complete audience attention
- The power of anticipation
- A room full of people willing you to succeed

And what do most speakers do with this gift? They squander it. They diffuse their power with meaningless movement, nervous gestures, and uncertain positioning. It's like being handed the keys to a Ferrari and choosing to push it down the street instead.

HERE'S YOUR NEW RULE: Enter. Plant. Connect. Power.

ENTER: Walk out with purpose. This isn't a casual stroll to get coffee—this is your moment. Take ownership of it.

PLANT: Find your power position (usually center stage, about 1/3 back from the front). Plant yourself there like you're growing roots into the stage. No shifting, no swaying, no nervous dance.

CONNECT: Take two or three seconds (yes, actually count them) to visually connect with different sections of your audience. Let them feel seen.

POWER: Then, and only then, deliver your opening line with absolute conviction.

I've seen speakers transform their entire presence with just this one change. A strong entrance doesn't just set up your first minute—it sets up your entire presentation.

What NOT to do:

- Don't immediately pace or wander
- Don't fidget or shift weight
- Don't rush to fill the silence
- Don't break your connection by looking down or away

Remember: Movement should be earned. Every step, every position change should have purpose. You'll have plenty of time to work the stage—but first, earn the right by owning your entrance.

Want to master this? Here's your homework:

1. Film yourself walking into a room and starting to speak
2. Watch it with the sound off
3. Ask yourself: "Would I trust this person with my attention?"
4. Practice your Enter-Plant-Connect-Power sequence until it feels as natural as breathing

Your first 30 seconds aren't just about starting your speech—they're about claiming your authority. Stop giving it away before you've even begun.

ACTION: Next time you're in an audience, watch how speakers enter. You'll start noticing the ones who own their power versus those who diffuse it. Then decide which one you want to be.

OVERCOMING PHYSICAL BARRIERS: BREAKING FREE FROM THE INVISIBLE STRAITJACKET

Okay, confession time. How many of you feel like you're wearing an invisible straitjacket when you present? You know, that feeling where your arms seem glued to your sides, your feet are stuck in cement, and your neck is stiffer than a two-day-old baguette?

We have all been there, like our bodies suddenly forget how to, well, body. But here's the thing—that disconnection from your physical self? It maintains a vice grip on your self-expression. And I'm here to help you break free from those invisible restraints. Consider me your Houdini of public speaking.

First things first, let's talk about why this happens. Fear, my friends. That pesky little emotion that makes us want to curl up into a ball and roll off stage. It blocks our energy flow tighter than a clogged drain. But unlike a clogged drain, we can't just pour some Drano down our throats and call it a day (please don't try that at home).

So how do you overcome this? How do you go from stiff as a board to flowing like water? Here are some tricks up my sleeve:

1. The Emotion Motion: Pick an emotion and try to express it using only your body. No words allowed. It is like the world's weirdest game of charades, but it helps you connect your emotions to your physical expression.
2. The Mirror, Mirror: Practice your presentation in front of a mirror. Watch your body language. If you look bored, your audience will feel bored. If you look excited, they'll perk up faster than a dog hearing a treat bag rustle.

3. The Grounding Game: Imagine roots growing from your feet into the ground. Feel the earth's energy flowing up through your body. It is like you're a human tree, but hopefully with better dance moves.
4. The Power Pose: Stand like Superman (or Superwoman) for two minutes before you present. Hands on hips, feet apart, chest out. It is scientifically proven to boost your confidence. Plus, you get to pretend you're a superhero. Win-win.
5. The Shake It Off: Before you go on stage, find a private spot and shake your whole body for thirty seconds. Yes, you'll look ridiculous. No, I don't care. It releases tension and gets your energy flowing.

Your goal isn't to become some robotic, perfectly poised speaker, but to let your authentic self shine through. Because that's what people connect with—the real, raw, human you.

Here is your final mission, should you choose to accept it (and you should):

Next time you're about to present, take a deep breath and ask yourself, "What would I do if I wasn't afraid?" Then do that. Move like that. Speak like that. Be that.

Because when you're fully alive in your body, when you're connected to your physical self, that's when the magic happens. That is when you stop giving a presentation and start telling a story. That is when you stop being a speaker and start being a force of nature.

So go forth, my physically liberated friends. Take up space. Move with purpose. Let your body speak as loudly as your words. You are not just delivering information—you're creating an experience. When you're fully embodied in your story, that's an experience your audience won't soon forget.

PHYSICALITY IN THE DIGITAL AGE: FROM PIXELS TO PRESENCE

Let's talk about the elephant in the Zoom room—how to translate your physical presence into the world of pixels and bandwidth. In this brave new world of virtual everything, if you can't own the Zoom, you can't own the room. (See what I did there? I'll be here all week, folks. Try the virtual veal!)

Sure, you've mastered the art of looking semi-professional from the waist up while wearing pajama pants. But there's a whole universe of digital physicality to explore. We're about to turn your online presence from "Can you hear me now?" to "Can you believe what you just saw?"

Camera-Ready: Mastering Physicality for Interviews

First stop on our digital tour: camera interviews. Whether you're Zooming with a potential employer or chatting with Anderson Cooper (hey, dream big!), these tips will have you looking like a seasoned pro.

1. Framing yourself: Think of the camera frame as your personal stage. You want to be the star, not a random extra. Position yourself slightly off-center (it's more visually interesting) and make sure there's a bit of space above your head. Nobody wants to see your scalp's origin story.
2. Eye contact 2.0: Remember how we talked about making eye contact? Well, now you need to make love to that camera lens. Okay, maybe not love. But at least a firm handshake. Look directly into the camera when speaking, not at the interviewer's face on your screen. It feels weird, but it looks great.

3. Gestures in limited space: Just because you're in a tiny rectangle doesn't mean you can't gesture. But keep them contained and purposeful. Think T-rex arms, but with more pizzazz.
4. Posture perils: Slouching is the silent killer of credibility. Sit up straight, but not so straight you look like you've swallowed a broomstick. Imagine a string pulling you up from the crown of your head. Now relax your shoulders. Perfect.

When I was in college for Broadcast Journalism at Drake University, we studied a bunch of major moments in TV journalism. One of the first we dissected was the infamous Nixon-Kennedy debate of 1960—a watershed moment that perfectly illustrates the power of visual presence in media.

On September 26, 1960, Senator John F. Kennedy and Vice President Richard Nixon squared off in the first-ever televised presidential debate. What happened next became a textbook example of how appearance can trump content in the world of visual media.

Nixon, who had been recently hospitalized and was still recovering, appeared pale, sickly, and sweaty under the harsh studio lights. He refused makeup, wore a grey suit that blended into the background, and sported a five o'clock shadow that made him look shifty. Kennedy, on the other hand, was the picture of youth and vitality: tanned, well-rested, and impeccably groomed.

The result? Those who listened to the debate on the radio largely thought Nixon had won. But the seventy million people who watched on TV? They overwhelmingly favored Kennedy. A survey by Sindlinger & Company showed that more than half of those who watched the debate on TV thought Kennedy had won, while those who listened on the radio gave Nixon the edge.

This historic moment underscores a crucial point: in visual media, how you look can be just as important as what you say. It isn't just about having the right answers; it's about presenting yourself in a way that exudes confidence, credibility, and charisma.

Fast forward to our era of Zoom calls and virtual interviews. While most of us aren't running for president, the principles remain the same. Your visual presence—how you frame yourself, your eye contact, your gestures, and your posture—all contribute to how you're perceived.

So, as you prepare for your next on-camera appearance, whether it's a job interview or a presentation to your team, remember the lesson of Nixon and Kennedy. Pay attention to your visual presence. Make sure your lighting flatters you (no sweaty upper lips, please). Choose clothing that pops against your background. And for goodness' sake, if someone offers you makeup, take it!

By mastering these elements of visual presence, you'll ensure your audience focuses on your message, not your appearance. And who knows? You might just win your own version of a presidential debate.

Social Media Swagger: Physicality for Short-Form Video

Welcome to the Wild West of content creation, where attention spans are shorter than a goldfish's and your competition is an endless stream of cat videos. Here is how to stand out:

The three-second rule: You have three seconds to capture attention. Use dynamic movement right off the bat. Start with a bold gesture, a dramatic lean into the camera, or even a (safe) jump cut.

Energy amplification: Remember how we said to dial up your energy for virtual presentations? For social media, crank that dial to eleven. You are competing with dancing teenagers and epic fail compilations. Bring the enthusiasm!

Movement hacks for vertical video: Vertical video is like a skinny hallway—not much room to move side to side, so work with up and down. Use levels—sit, stand, crouch. And don't be afraid to get close to the camera for emphasis.

Facial expressions: In a world of silent autoplay, your face needs to do the talking. Exaggerate your expressions. Think Jim Carrey, but maybe dial it back juuust a bit.

VIRTUAL VIRTUOSO: PHYSICALITY FOR ONLINE SPEECHES AND PRESENTATIONS

Alright, digital divas and virtual virtuosos, it's time to turn your webcam into your personal Broadway stage. This goes beyond "unmute yourself" territory. It means transforming that little rectangle on the screen into a portal of engagement that rivals the *Stranger Things'* Upside Down in its ability to captivate an audience (but with fewer demogorgons and more charisma).

RETHINKING THE VIRTUAL STAGE

First things first—forget everything you think you know about being stationary on camera: You're not a hostage video, you're a dynamic presenter! Just because you're confined to a screen doesn't mean you have to be a talking head.

Think of your frame as a stage. You wouldn't stand in one spot on a physical stage, so why do it on a virtual one? Move, people! Lean in, step back, use your space. Create a set that allows for movement. Maybe it's a standing desk setup, or perhaps it's just pushing that pile of laundry out of frame (we've all been there). The point is, give yourself room to be the vibrant, movement-filled presenter you are.

The Camera as Your Dance Partner

Work that camera like it's the last dance at prom (but with less awkward swaying and more purposeful movement).

Remember proxemics? That fancy term for how we use space in communication? Well, it's time to apply it to your virtual world. When you want to emphasize a point, lean into the camera like you're telling the audience a secret. They'll lean in too.

Want to give them some perspective? Take a step back. It is the virtual equivalent of a mic drop, minus the risk of actually dropping expensive audio equipment.

The key is to vary your distance. It keeps your audience engaged and prevents them from mistaking your presentation for a particularly boring episode of *The Brady Bunch.*

FRAMING FOR CONNECTION

Forget everything you've read about framing yourself for virtual presentations. That head-and-shoulders-only advice? As outdated as dial-up internet.

Here is the secret sauce: frame yourself from the waist up. Why? Because you're not talking to a room full of people anymore but to *one* person, who's probably sitting alone, wondering if they have time to microwave a burrito before the next meeting.

According to anthropologist Edward Hall (the godfather of proxemics), Americans prefer a distance of eighteen inches to four feet when talking to each other. Translate that to your screen, and you've got a waist-up shot. This not only mimics a natural conversation but also gives you room to gesture. And let's be honest, what's a good story without some wild hand movements?

Competing with Distractions

A harsh truth: when you present virtually, you're not just competing with other screens. You are up against notifications, pets, kids, spouses, roommates, coworkers, and the siren call of an Amazon delivery.

Your job? Be as engaging as their favorite binge-worthy TV show. No pressure, right?

This is why you must bring your whole physical presence to the party. Use your facial expressions, your gestures, your movement. Be so engaging that they forget all about that pile of laundry in the corner (the same one you pushed out of frame earlier).

Energy Amplification for Virtual Spaces

Here is a fun experiment: record yourself giving a presentation with your normal energy level. Now watch it back. Feel a bit... underwhelmed? The camera eats energy for breakfast, lunch, and dinner.

In the virtual world, you need to amplify your energy. Do not become a caricature of yourself, but definitely turn it up a notch. Or three. Think of it as the difference between theater acting and film acting, but in reverse. You need to project to the back row of a theater that happens to be watching on a thirteen-inch laptop screen.

Virtual Eye Contact: Through the Looking Glass

Ah, eye contact. The holy grail of connection. But how do you make eye contact with a little black dot without looking like you're either auditioning for a zombie apocalypse movie or trying to win a staring contest with your webcam?

Welcome to what I call the *Through the Looking Glass* technique. Think of Alice stepping through the mirror into

Wonderland. Your job is to look not at the camera lens, but through it, to the wonderland of your audience beyond.

Many people get eye contact wrong in two spectacularly creepy ways:

1. The Dead-Eyed Stare: They focus on the actual glass of the lens, giving them all the warmth and personality of a mannequin in a forgotten department store window.
2. The Serial Killer Gaze: They never break eye contact, staring relentlessly into the lens like they're trying to set it on fire with their mind.

Neither of these is going to win you any virtual presentation awards (unless "Most Likely to Make the Audience Check Their Locks" is a category).

Action:

Look out a window and shift your gaze from focusing on the glass to looking at what's beyond. Feel how your eyes change? That's the magic we're after. Now apply that same principle to your camera. Look *not* at the lens but *through* it to your imaginary audience on the other side. Better yet—make that imaginary audience *one single person* you are trying to connect with.

But wait, there's more! (I feel like an infomercial host, but stick with me.) In real-life conversations, we don't maintain constant eye contact. The person speaking might look up to think or to the side to make a connection, while the listener maintains more consistent eye contact. Your job is to mimic this natural rhythm in your virtual presentations.

So, when you make a key point, sure, make "eye contact" with the camera. But don't be afraid to look away naturally as you would in a regular conversation. Glance at your notes, look up in thought, and match your eyes to the message you are delivering to create that likeness of a natural, engaging conversation.

If all else fails, this trick never fails to bring a smile: stick a tiny googly eye on either side of your camera lens. It is an instant connection maker, plus it's hilarious. Nothing breaks the ice quite like a presenter trying not to giggle at a googly eye.

Your goal isn't really to make love to the camera (please don't, that's a whole different kind of video), but to make your audience feel like they're having a natural, engaging conversation with you. Channel your inner Alice, step through that looking glass, and take your audience on a journey to your own personal Wonderland of ideas. Just watch out for the Jabberwocky. I hear he gives terrible presentation advice.

Gesturing for Impact: The Silent Language of the Hands

Being virtual doesn't mean your hands should take a vacation. In fact, they should be working overtime! But here's the catch—you need to keep them within the frame, like playing charades but with a purpose.

Think of your gestures as visual punctuation marks. They should enhance your words, not distract from them. A well-timed hand movement can underscore a key point more effectively than a dozen PowerPoint slides.

Action:

Next time you emphasize a crucial idea, use the "box" gesture. Make a box shape with your hands to visually "contain" your concept, like you're gift-wrapping your ideas for your audience. Just don't actually wrap yourself—that's a different kind of performance art.

Voice and Physicality in Harmony: The Dynamic Duo

Your voice and body should be best friends, not awkward strangers at a party. They should be finishing each other's sentences, high-fiving, and generally being in perfect sync.

Match your vocal energy to your physical energy. If you lean in to make an important point, let your voice reflect that intensity. If you step back to give a broader perspective, let your voice expand to fill that space.

Action:

Try this fun exercise: Deliver the same sentence with different physical and vocal combinations. Say, "This is important," while slouching and speaking softly. Now say it while standing tall and projecting your voice. Feel the difference? This is the power of harmony between voice and physicality.

Setting the Virtual Stage: Your Background's Time to Shine

Your background is the supporting actor in your presentation—it should enhance your performance, not steal the show. It is the Robin to your Batman, the Watson to your Sherlock, the... well, you get the idea.

Choose a background that's professional but not boring. A blank wall is safe, but about as exciting as watching paint dry. A bookshelf can add depth and personality, but make sure those book titles are ones you're happy for people to see. (No *Virtual Presentations for Dummies*, please!)

And for the love of all that is holy, check what's visible before you start. We have all seen enough embarrassing Zoom backgrounds to last a lifetime. Nobody needs to see your collection of garden gnomes or that pile of laundry you've been avoiding. Unless, of course, you're giving a presentation on procrastination—in which case, carry on.

> **Pro tip:** Test your lighting. You want to be bathed in the glow of competence, not look like you're auditioning for a horror movie.

ENGAGING THE INVISIBLE AUDIENCE: CONDUCTING THE VIRTUAL SYMPHONY

Presenting to a screen can feel like talking to a void, as if you're the last person on Earth giving a TED talk to an audience of houseplants. But remember, there are real people on the other side. They're not just pixels—they're Stuart from accounting, Kris from marketing, and that guy from IT whose name you can never remember (sorry, guy from IT).

Use physical cues to guide their attention. Point to where you want them to look. Use your facial expressions to signal how they should feel. Be the conductor of their viewing experience. If you look excited, they'll perk up. If you look bored... they might suddenly remember some urgent emails they need to check.

Action:

Use the "spotlight" technique. When you make a key point, lean slightly into the camera and use both hands to create a "spotlight" gesture, as if you're shining a light on your most important idea. You are saying, "Hey, wake up! This is the good stuff!" without actually having to say it. You can do the same thing by pretending you are leaning in to tell them a secret.

Your goal is to make your virtual presentation so engaging that your audience forgets they're watching through a screen. You want them so captivated they don't even notice their cat walk across the keyboard or their kids stage a coup in the background. The bar is pretty low when it comes to engagement during virtual presentations—so you will be stepping into Academy Award Winning PowerPoint territory with these ideas.

Mastering virtual presentations is more than knowing which button to click to share your screen. Use every tool in your physical toolbox to break through the digital barrier and create a connection. Turn that little webcam into a window of opportunity, a portal of engagement, a... okay, I'm running out of metaphors here, but you get the idea.

So go forth, my virtual virtuosos. Make that webcam your stage, that background your set, and that invisible audience your rapt admirers. When you nail a virtual presentation, it's not just a win for you, it's a win for everyone who doesn't have to sit through another monotonous monologue delivered by a talking head. If that's not a public service, I don't know what is.

In the world of virtual presentations, physicality isn't just about what you do with your body, but how you use your entire presence to connect, engage, and yes, *own* the Zoom. When you can turn a pixelated rectangle into a stage, you know you've truly mastered the art of digital physicality.

Now, if you'll excuse me, I need to go practice my, "leaning in dramatically while not knocking over my laptop" technique. It's harder than it looks.

Cross-Platform Physicality: Maintaining Consistency Across Mediums

You aren't just a one-trick pony, are you? Of course not! *You* are a multi-platform superstar. But how do you maintain a consistent physical presence across all these mediums? Glad you asked!

- Developing your physical brand: Just like you have a personal brand, you need a physical brand. Are you the energetic hand-talker? The calm, collected presence? The dramatic pauser? Figure out your signature moves and use them consistently.
- Adapting energy levels: Different platforms require different energy levels. Think of it like a volume knob. Social media might be at a nine, virtual presentations at a seven, and one-on-one interviews at a five. But the underlying "sound"—that's you—stays the same.
- Translating in-person charisma to digital spaces: Your in-person charm might not automatically translate to digital. Practice, practice, practice. Record yourself and watch it back. It might be painful, but it's the fastest way to improve.

Tech-Savvy Body Language: Incorporating New Technologies

Buckle up, space cowboys. We're headed to the future!

Physicality for augmented reality presentations: Imagine giving a presentation where you can pull 3D models out of thin air. Cool, right? But it also means mastering a whole new set of gestures. Start practicing your "swipe," "pinch," and "expand" movements now.

Body language in the age of holograms and virtual reality: One day, we might give presentations as full-body holograms or in virtual reality environments. The rules of physicality will change again. Will we need to learn how to make our avatars' body language match our words? Only time will tell.

Remember, folks, no matter how advanced the technology gets, your goal remains the same: to connect with your audience. Whether you beam yourself into their living room as a hologram or just wave at them through a webcam, it's all about using your physical presence to enhance your message. We've covered the first three of the Five Stage Lanugages – Verbal, Vocal, and Physical – and now we move into the fourth: the Visual Langauge.

** Don't forget to check out:
www.mikeganino.com/bookresources
to grab a free embodiment practice to help you bring your physicality to life. **

VISUAL
CRAYONS
LANGUAGE

CHAPTER 7

THE WES ANDERSON EFFECT: MASTERING THE VISUAL LANGUAGE

(OR HOW TO MAKE YOUR POWERPOINT MORE AESTHETIC THAN A TWEE HIPSTER'S INSTAGRAM)

> *"To me, style is just the outside of content, and content the inside of style, like the outside and the inside of the human body—both go together, they can't be separated."*
>
> **— Jean-Luc Godard, French Film Director**

You are in a dimly lit theater, the smell of popcorn wafting through the air. Suddenly, the screen explodes with color—perfect symmetry, meticulous details, and a color palette that makes you want to repaint your entire house. You've just been Wes Anderson-ed.

I am not suggesting you start wearing berets and speaking in deadpan (unless that's your thing, in which case, rock on). But what if I told you that channeling a bit of that Wes Anderson magic could transform your presentations from "meh" to "magnificent"? We are about to dive into the world of visual language, where every slide, prop, and carefully chosen outfit turns you into the director of your own communication masterpiece.

First, let's talk about crutches—not the ones that support you when you've broken your leg after too many Aperol Spritz on the narrow streets of Venice but the ones we use that keep us from expressing our truth. You know what I'm talking about. Those densely packed PowerPoint slides that make your audience's eyes glaze over faster than a donut at Krispy Kreme. The ones that scream, "I'm terrified I'll forget something, so I've written a novel on each slide!"

You are enough. Yes, you. Without the crutches, without the endless bullet points, without the clip art that went out of style sometime in the last millennium. You have a story to tell, and guess what? It isn't hiding in those slides. It's in you.

I learned this lesson the hard way. Picture it: A theater rented out, camera crew ready, and me—armed with a bloated 174-slide deck for a fifteen-minute talk. Why? Because somewhere along the line, I'd convinced myself that more slides meant more value. Spoiler alert: It doesn't. All it means is more opportunities for your audience to check their phones or plan their grocery lists. The slide deck kept me focused on what was coming next in the presentation and kept me from really connecting with the audience. The video I got from that day has not seen the light of day.

Visual language isn't just about what happens on stage or in a boardroom. In today's world, it's about every pixel you put out there. It is the Instagram story you posted this morning, the Zoom background you chose for your virtual meeting, and yes, even the outfit you picked for your LinkedIn profile picture.

This chapter explores how to harness the power of visual storytelling across all these platforms. You will learn how to turn slides from crutches into creative canvases, how to use props that pop (without looking like you're auditioning for a magician's assistant), and how to create a visual brand as unmistakable as Wes Anderson's symmetrical shots.

You will dive into the world of virtual presentations, where "owning the Zoom" is the new "owning the room." If you've never thought of yourself as a visual person, get ready for a shift in perspective. By the end of this chapter, you'll see the world through a new lens, one where every visual choice is an opportunity to enhance your message.

So, are you ready to turn your communication into a visual feast that would make even the most discerning film critic nod in approval? Grab your metaphorical director's chair, and let's get started. It is time to create your own grand visual masterpiece—no quirky soundtrack required (but hey, if you've got one, I won't judge).

SLIDES: FROM CRUTCH TO CREATIVE CANVAS

Ah, slides. The comfort blanket of presenters everywhere. The thing we cling to like toddlers to their favorite stuffed animals at bedtime. You might think you need to cram every pixel with information to prove your expertise. (Spoiler alert: you don't.) It's time to turn your slide deck from a security blanket into a magic carpet ride. This is what I call The Mainstage Slide Strategy, and it will become your new blueprint for standing ovation-worthy slide decks.

The "Death by PowerPoint" Phenomenon: A Tragedy in Multiple Acts

We've all been there. Sitting in a dimly lit room, watching slide after slide of bullet points march across the screen like ants at a picnic. There isn't even enough contrast between the color of the slide background and the color of the fonts. You can't read it properly. Your eyes glaze over, your mind wanders, and suddenly you're planning your entire weekend, including a detailed grocery list and the optimal route to avoid traffic. Congratulations, you've just experienced "Death by PowerPoint."

PowerPoint (or Keynote, or Prezi, or whatever your slide poison of choice is) *isn't* the killer. It is just the weapon. We, my friends, are the perpetrators. We are the ones stuffing slides with enough text to rival *War and Peace*, thinking, "If I put it on the slide, I can't forget it!"

News flash: If you need to read your slides to remember your content, you might want to consider a career in professional slide-reading. ***(Not a real job. I checked.)***

Breaking Free From the Slide Crutch: Your Content Rehab Program

Step 1: Admit you have a problem. "Hi, I'm [Your Name], and I'm addicted to overcrowded slides."

Step 2: Embrace the blank slide. Yes, it's scary. Yes, it feels like staring into the void. But that void is full of possibilities.

Step 3: Ask yourself, "What would Wes do?" Would he cram seventeen bullet points onto a beige background? Or would he create a visually striking image that tells a story at a glance?

I once worked with a client—let's call her Stephanie (because that was her name) —who came to me with a two-hundred-slide deck for a thirty-minute presentation. Two hundred slides. That is a new slide every nine seconds. Unless you're running some kind of twisted "speed sliding" competition, that's overkill.

We sat down, and I asked her one simple question: "If your slides burst into flames right before your presentation, what would you say?"

She looked at me like I'd just suggested we present in our underwear. But then, something magical happened. She started talking. And you know what? She knew her stuff. She was passionate, knowledgeable, and engaging. The slides didn't add to her presentation; they took away from it.

By the time we finished, her deck was down to fifteen slides. Fifteen. And each one was a visual feast that enhanced her words instead of replacing them. The result? Standing ovation. (Okay, a seated ovation because it was a corporate gig, but you could feel the standing ovation energy in the room.)

The New Rules of Slide Club:

1. Your slides are not your script. They are the backup singers to your lead vocal.
2. If you can say it better than the slide can show it, say it.
3. Think of each slide as a movie poster for your idea. It should intrigue, not explain.
4. Embrace white space. It is not your enemy; it's the breath your audience needs to absorb your brilliance.
5. Use high-quality, relevant images. No more clip art from 1997, Karen. Make sure these images are either full bleed (meaning the reach all four edges of the screen) or are framed in some way (if you have a

vertical picture that can't be stretched without losing quality, then use a mockup to place that image inside a frame or smart phone).

6. Font size should be visible from space. Or at least from the back of the room. You want thick, easy to read fonts. I know you may have a cool script font that is part of your brand, but if the audience struggles to read it, then it isn't serving your speech.
7. Color contrast is your friend. Unless you're going for that, "I can't read this, so I'll just nap," vibe. You want your font and your background color to high contrast, and keep in mind that overhead lighting can impact the readability of your slides.

The Question Deck: Turning Monologue Into Dialogue

Try this revolutionary idea: What if your slides asked questions instead of giving answers? I call this the "Question Deck" approach, and it's a game-changer.

Instead of a slide that says "Our Q3 Sales Increased by 27%," try, "What do you think happened to our Q3 sales?" Boom. You've just turned your audience from passive slide-readers into engaged participants.

I used this technique with a CEO who was, let's say, enthusiastically attached to his data-heavy slides. By the end of our session, he had a deck that not only engaged his board but got them asking questions and contributing ideas. He went from "Spreadsheet Steve" to "Storytelling Stefan" in one presentation. As we've discussed, every presentation should feel like an exchange and not a pedantic lecture.

Remember, your slides are not a crutch. Nor are they a cheat sheet. They are a visual accompaniment to your rock star performance. Use them to amplify your message, not to replace it.

So, the next time you're tempted to create a slide with more bullet points than a Wild West shootout, stop. Take a deep breath. And ask yourself: "What would Wes do?"

Your audience will thank you. And who knows? You might just start a visual revolution. No color-coded berets required.

DIRECTOR'S CUT: THE SLIDELESS OPENING GAMBIT

You're about to give the presentation of your life to two thousand eager faces. You step on stage, click your remote, and... nothing. The screen stays blank. Suddenly, you're sweating more than a long-tailed cat in a room full of rocking chairs. Sound familiar?

This pro tip will save your bacon (and your dignity): Always have a few minutes of killer content that doesn't rely on slides.

Technology is as reliable as a chocolate teapot. But you know what never crashes? Your voice and your stories.

Here is my secret sauce:

1. Start with your cover slide.
2. Follow it with a blank "holding" slide.
3. Launch into your opening story while this blank slide is up.

This strategy is smoother than a fresh jar of Skippy. If your slides work, great! If not, you'll know the moment you click to that blank slide. But here's the kicker—your audience won't have a clue. They'll be too busy hanging on your every word.

After you've charmed their socks off for a few minutes, casually check in with the AV team. Something like, "So, shall we dive in? Oh, and AV team, it looks like I might've accidentally muted my slides or something. Can you help me reconnect?"

Remember, the show must go on—with or without slides. And a great story beats a bullet point any day of the week.

PROPS: BRINGING YOUR MESSAGE TO LIFE

Hey there, prop stars (see what I did there?), let's talk about the unsung heroes of the presentation world. Not the AV team who miraculously fixes your tech issues two minutes before you go on stage (though they are heroes, no doubt). I mean props—those tangible, touchable, sometimes-fall-apart-at-the-worst-moment objects that can turn your presentation from "meh" to "memorable."

The Power of the Prop: More Than Just Fancy Show-and-Tell

Think back to your school days. Remember how exciting it was when a teacher brought in something real to illustrate a point? Suddenly, that boring history lesson about ancient Egypt came to life because Mrs Wilson brought in a (probably fake) mummy's hand. That is the power of props, folks.

In the world of presentations, a well-chosen prop can be the difference between your audience checking their watches and them leaning in so far they're practically on stage with you.

Prop Stars: When Objects Become Legends

Let's look at some prop superstars who've nailed the art of object integration:

1. Bill Gates and the Mosquitoes: In a TED talk about malaria, Gates released a jar of mosquitoes into the audience. Talk about buzz-worthy content! (They weren't infected. Gates may be passionate, but he's not homicidal.)
2. Jamie Oliver's Sugar Avalanche: To illustrate the amount of sugar consumed by children, Oliver

dumped a wheelbarrow full of sugar cubes on stage. Suddenly, statistics became shockingly tangible.

3. Hans Rosling's Washing Machine: In a talk about global development, Rosling brought out a washing machine to demonstrate its impact on education and gender equality. Who knew laundry could be so enlightening?
4. Monica Lewinsky's Powerful Podium: In her 2015 TED talk "The Price of Shame," Lewinsky used the podium—typically shunned in TED presentations—as a powerful prop. She stood behind it for most of her talk, symbolizing how she had hidden from public view for years. But in a dramatic moment at the end, as she declared, "I've decided to take back my narrative," she stepped out from behind the podium. This simple yet powerful use of a prop perfectly embodied her message of reclaiming her story and facing the world on her own terms.

My client, Neen James, is one of the world's experts on the luxury marketplace. In her keynote, we've crafted a playful yet impactful story about Barbe-Nicole Ponsardin—the woman known today as The Widow Clicquot and founder of that famous orange-labeled Champagne Vueve Clicquot. In the talk, she has a bottle of Vueve on a table on stage, and at some point she picks up the bottle to show the audience the image of Madame Clicquot that is on the top of each muselet—the little cage that holds the cork in. She references the bottle a few times, and then (when possible) gives the bottle away at the end of her talk to an audience volunteer. Neen also has a muselet charm on her necklace which she references at the end when she asks the audience to consider the "cages" they and their brands find themselves in. These uses of the props (both the bottle and the necklace) are brilliant and also help carry the throughline from her opening story all the way to the end of the talk.

The *Dos* and *Don'ts* of Prop Mastery

Dos:

1. Keep it relevant: Your prop should illustrate your point, not distract from it. Your collection of rare Pez dispensers probably isn't relevant to your sales strategy presentation.
2. Practice, practice, practice: Nothing kills a moment like fumbling with your prop. Unless fumbling is part of your bit, in which case, fumble away!
3. Make it visible: If your audience needs binoculars to see your prop, it might as well be invisible.
4. Have a backup plan: Props can be fickle creatures. Always be ready to describe your prop if it decides to go rogue.

Don'ts:

1. Don't let it upstage you: You are the star, not your prop. Unless you're a ventriloquist, in which case, carry on.
2. Avoid anything alive: Remember Bill Gates? Yeah, don't do that unless you're, well, Bill Gates.
3. Skip the cheese factor: A prop should enhance your message, not make your audience groan. (Looking at you, guy-who-brings-a-rubber-chicken-to-every-presentation.)
4. Don't overdo it: Using a prop for every point is like adding bacon to every dish. Delicious in theory, but in practice... moderation is key.

The Unexpected Prop: When Your Environment Becomes Your Ally

Pro tip: Sometimes the best props are the ones you don't bring with you. Use your environment creatively.

I once saw a speaker use the hotel lobby's revolving door to illustrate customer churn. Every time someone walked through, he'd say, "There goes another one!" By the end of his talk, the audience couldn't look at that door without thinking about retention strategies.

The Virtual Prop Challenge: Bringing Tangibility to the Digital World

Now, about virtual presentations. You might be thinking you can't exactly reach through the screen and hand your audience a prop. (If you figure out how to do that, please let me know. I've got some Netflix snacks I'd like to share.)

In the virtual world, props become even more crucial. They break up the monotony of talking heads and shared screens. Here are some ideas:

1. **The Show-and-Tell Approach**: Hold up objects to the camera. Just make sure your video quality is good, or you might end up looking like you're wielding a mysterious blob.
2. **The Digital Prop**: Use digital tools to create interactive elements. Think polls, word clouds, or even simple animations.
3. **The Prop Hunt:** Send your audience on a quick scavenger hunt in their own space. "Find something blue that represents our company values!" It is engaging and gets them moving—win-win!
4. **The Real Thing:** Instead of showing slides of pictures or objects, just have actual pictures and objects to share. Imagine the impact if you shared a framed photo of your favorite poodle versus just adding it to your slide deck.

Whether you're on stage or on screen, props are your secret weapon in the battle against boredom. Use them wisely, and you'll not only capture your audience's attention—you might just capture their imaginations too.

INTERACTIVE VISUALS: FLIP CHARTS AND REAL-TIME DRAWING

Picassos of the presentation world, let's channel your inner kindergartener and embrace the power of drawing. I don't suggest you start your next board meeting by passing out crayons and construction paper (although, let's be honest, that would be awesome). I am talking about the magic of flip charts and real-time drawing.

The Power of the Pen: Why Scribbling Beats Clicking

In a world of slick PowerPoint transitions and AI-generated graphics, there's something refreshingly human about watching someone draw, like watching Bob Ross create a happy little tree, except instead of a landscape, you get a picture of your quarterly sales projections. (Hey, every spreadsheet needs a friend, right?)

Flip Chart Fundamentals: More Than Just Giant Post-It Notes

Flip charts are the trusted tool of the presentation world: versatile, always ready, and in a pinch, you can use them to fan yourself if the AC breaks down. But beyond their emergency cooling capabilities, flip charts have some serious presentation superpowers:

1. Attention Magnets: When you start drawing, people can't help but watch. It is like a mini-performance art piece, except with more bar graphs and fewer interpretive dances about the human condition.
2. Flexible: Unlike slides, flip charts let you adapt on the fly. Audience member has a brilliant idea? Boom,

it's on the chart. Your market projections were a bit optimistic? No problem, just draw that line trending down instead of up. (Maybe add a sad face for effect.)

3. Collaborative: Flip charts invite participation. Hand that marker over and suddenly your presentation becomes a group art project. Just be prepared for that one person who thinks they're Banksy.
4. Tech-Proof: No Wi-Fi? Power outage? Solar flare knocked out all electronics? No problem. Your trusty flip chart is ready to save the day.

The Art of Real-Time Drawing: It's Not About Being Picasso

If you're worried about your artistic abilities—maybe you can't even draw a straight line with a ruler—fear not. The beauty of real-time drawing isn't about creating a masterpiece—it's about engaging your audience and illustrating your ideas both literally and figuratively.

Here are some tips to make your scribbles more scintillating:

1. Embrace the Stick Figure: Simple is often better. Your audience doesn't expect Michelangelo; they just want to understand your point.
2. Use Color Strategically: Different colors can help categorize ideas or highlight important points. Just don't go overboard, or your flip chart might look like a tie-dye experiment gone wrong.
3. Practice Basic Shapes: Circles, squares, triangles—master these, and you can draw anything. Well, anything vaguely geometric, anyway.
4. Learn Some Visual Vocabulary: Arrows, speech bubbles, stars—these simple shapes can add a lot of meaning to your drawings.

5. When in Doubt, Label It: If your tree looks more like a broccoli floret, just label it "tree." Problem solved!

The Virtual Flip Chart: Bringing Doodles to the Digital Age

You might be thinking you can't exactly ship a flip chart to everyone's home office for those virtual presentations (Not with that attitude, you can't!). More practically, there are some great digital tools that can bring the flip chart experience to the virtual world:

1. Digital Whiteboards: Tools like Miro or Mural let you create virtual flip charts that your audience can even collaborate on in real time. It is like a multiplayer drawing game, but with more ROI and fewer alien invasions.
2. Tablet Drawing: With a tablet and stylus, you can draw directly onto your shared screen. It is like being John Madden, but instead of football plays, you're diagramming your company's five-year plan.
3. Annotation Tools: Most video conferencing platforms have built-in annotation tools. They might not be as fancy as a real marker, but they get the job done. Plus, you don't have to worry about marker stains on your shirt.

Whether you wield a marker or a stylus, your goal is the same: engage your audience, illustrate your ideas, and maybe unleash your inner child who always wanted to draw on the walls. (Do not draw on the walls. Most venues frown upon that.)

Well, Dear Reader, that's all the doodling wisdom I have for now. Time to cap this marker and roll up this flip chart. But

I'll be back faster than you can say "permanent ink on a white shirt." (**Pro tip:** Always keep a spare shirt handy or wear black. Trust me on this one.)

ATTIRE: DRESSING AS A VISUAL EXTENSION OF YOUR MESSAGE

Fashion mavens and style novices alike, we need to address a major fashion faux pas. Not that guy in the back wearing a Hawaiian shirt to a board meeting (though we'll get to him). I am talking about your attire—that visual handshake you give your audience before you even open your mouth.

Now, I'm not here to turn you into the next *Drag Race* winner (though if that happens, I expect at least a footnote in your Emmy award nomination speech), but to help you understand that what you wear isn't just about looking good—it's about enhancing your message and connecting with your audience.

The Power of the Visual Handshake

Your outfit is like the opening credits of a movie. It sets the tone, gives a hint of what's to come, and if done right, gets people excited for the main event. Done wrong, you're that Netflix show everyone skips the intro for.

Pro Tip: Let's talk about something no one warns you about but many experience—the pre-show nervous pee. After one too many encounters with wet bathroom counters and the dreaded post-urinal drippage (you know what I'm talking about), I've learned my lesson. Ever tried to discretely use a hand dryer on your crotch while praying the event planner who hired you doesn't walk in? Not my finest moment. Now I have an ironclad rule: dark pants on stage. Always. Black or navy blue are your friends. This is the kind of hard-won wisdom they don't teach you in public speaking class, folks. You're welcome. (And sorry for the TMI—but someone had to say it!)

Dressing for Your Audience: Know Your Crowd

There is no one-size-fits-all approach to presentation attire. The key is to know your audience. Are you speaking to a room full of Silicon Valley tech bros? A bunch of Wall Street suits? A gathering of creative types who consider mismatched socks a fashion statement?

Your goal is to be one notch *above* your audience's typical attire. Why? Because you want to look polished and professional, but not so out of place that your clothes become a distraction.

- For the tech crowd: Think "smart casual." Like you care, but not too much.
- For the finance folks: Break out that power suit. But maybe leave the Gordon Gekko suspenders at home.
- For the creatives: Have fun, but remember, there's a fine line between "artistic flair" and "escaped circus performer."

Color Me Impressed: The Psychology of Color

Colors aren't just for making pretty rainbows. They can influence how your audience perceives you and your message. Here is a quick rundown:

- **Blue:** Trustworthy and calm. Great for when you're trying to convince everyone that those Q4 numbers aren't as bad as they look.
- **Red:** Powerful and energetic. Perfect for that motivational speech about crushing your goals (and your enemies... I mean, competitors).
- **Green:** Growth and harmony. Ideal for pitching your new eco-friendly, definitely-not-a-pyramid-scheme business opportunity.

- **Black:** Sophisticated and authoritative. When you need to channel your inner James Bond (minus the martini and exploding pen).
- **White:** Clean and simple. Great for when you want to look pure and innocent (like when explaining why the office coffee budget tripled last month).
- **Purple:** Luxury and creativity. Perfect for when you want everyone to forget you're presenting from your garage and pretend you're in a corner office.
- **Yellow:** Optimistic and energetic. Use this when you need to convince the team that working weekends is actually "a growth opportunity." You can see this gorgeously applied to Laura Gassner Otting's growth-focused book *Limitless.*
- **Orange:** Friendly and confident. Great for when you want to seem approachable but still remind everyone you're the boss.
- **Pink:** Nurturing and compassionate. Ideal for delivering bad news, like explaining why the office snack budget now only covers rice cakes.
- **Brown:** Reliable and grounded. When you need everyone to believe you definitely know what you're talking about (even if you're secretly Googling under the podium).
- **Gray:** Professional and neutral. For those times when you want to blend into the background like a corporate ninja.

DIRECTOR'S CUT

Colors mean different things in different cultures. So before you go all-in on white for your presentation, remember it's associated with mourning in places like China, Japan, and India. Maybe check that before you accidentally turn your product launch into what looks like a funeral.

Whatever color you choose, make sure it offers a pleasing contrast (rather than a painful clash) with your background. You don't want to disappear like a chameleon on a PowerPoint slide.

Accessories: The Spice of Life (and Presentations)

Accessories are like the garnish on a fancy cocktail: they're not the main event, but they can certainly elevate the experience. Just remember:

- Less is more. Go for, "successful professional," not, "walking jewelry store."
- Choose accessories that serve a purpose. A watch? Practical. A monocle? Unless you're doing a Sherlock Holmes impersonation, maybe leave that one at home.

- If it makes noise, lose it. Nothing kills a dramatic pause like the jingle-jangle of your lucky charm bracelet. Also—if you are wearing a lav mic, those fancy necklaces can create unwanted sound.

The Virtual Wardrobe: Dressing for the Camera

In our brave new world of virtual presentations, level up your attire game. Here are some quick tips:

- Avoid patterns that make the camera go wonky. Unless causing medical grade dizziness is part of your presentation strategy.
- Only half of you is visible. So go ahead, pair that crisp button-down with your favorite sweatpants. Just don't stand up mid-presentation if the camera will highlight your Lululemons.
- Contrast is key. You don't want to blend into your background like some kind of corporate chameleon. If the walls behind you are white, wear a darker top. If the walls behind you are black, wear a lighter top.

One of my clients (who shall remain nameless) had a t-shirt with the Pablo Picasso dachshund on it. You know, those adorable little weiner dogs that look like little German sausages with legs. Super cute, and totally in resonance with the event and theme of her message. But she tossed on a smart blazer which made the head and the tail of the dog disappear but still showed just enough of the legs of the dog on both sides to make it look like her shirt was... well... a different kind of weiner. So, Dear Reader, if you have any graphics on your shirt, please double-check the final look before you take the stage. In the words of Jennifer Coolidge in *Legally Blonde 2*, "makes me want a hot dog real bad."

The Bottom Line on Bottomless Style

At the end of the day, the best outfit is one that makes you feel confident and aligns with your message. If you feel good, you'll present well. Just remember: no matter how great your outfit is, it's not a substitute for preparation. A $5,000 suit won't save a $5 presentation.

So go forth, you stylish presenters. Dress to impress, align with your message, and for the love of all that is holy, double-check your zipper before you take the stage. Even the most dazzling accessories can't distract from some wardrobe malfunctions.

Now, if you need me, I'll be color-coordinating my Apple Watch band collection with my slide deck backgrounds. You know, just in case Wes Anderson decides to direct my next speech.

SOCIAL MEDIA VISUALS: CRAFTING YOUR DIGITAL AESTHETIC

Welcome to the Wild West of content creation, where attention spans are shorter than a goldfish's and your competition is an endless stream of cat videos and dance challenges. We're about to turn your social media feed from "meh" into "more, please!"

The Instagram Effect: More Than Just Filters and Faux-Candids

Remember when Instagram was all about making your lunch look like it was shot by Annie Leibovitz? Well, times have changed, and now it's about making your entire life look like it's straight from the set of *The Royal Tenenbaums* (see what I did there?). But fear not, you don't need a symmetry-obsessed cinematographer to create scroll-stopping content.

Location, Location, Location: Turning Your World into a Content Studio

News flash: You don't need a fancy studio to create great content. Your world is your studio. That coffee shop you work from? That's your set. The park you walk through? That's your backdrop. Your messy desk? That's... well, maybe clean it up first, but then it's content gold!

Here is how to make the most of your surroundings:

1. The Coffee Shop Confessional: Use that artisanal latte as a prop while you drop knowledge bombs about your industry. Just don't dunk your phone in it while trying to get the perfect shot.

2. The Park Podcast: Take your content outside. Nature makes a great backdrop, and the occasional squirrel cameo can only improve your engagement rates.
3. The Office Odyssey: Turn your workspace into a content playground. That stack of books? A visual representation of your learning journey. That plant you've somehow kept alive? A metaphor for growth. That overflowing trash can? A... reminder to clean up before shooting.

My client, Jacquette M. Timmons, is a New Yorker through and through. She uses the city as a backdrop for her walk-and-talk style videos, as inspiration for content (like the time she used a condo for sale to talk about financial planning), and to help frame her perspective by giving the viewers a location to place all the action in her videos (compare that to a boring talking head video against a white backdrop).

Props: Not Just for Theatre Kids Anymore

Remember when we talked about props in presentations? Well, in the social media world, everything is a prop. And I mean *everything.*

1. The Bookshelf Backdrop: Nothing says, "I'm intellectual, but in a cool way," like a strategically arranged bookshelf. Bonus points if you can sneak in a few guilty pleasure reads among the classics.
2. The Tech Stack: Arrange your devices like you're about to hack into the Matrix. It doesn't matter if you're actually just checking email, it looks impressive.
3. The Whiteboard Wonder: Scribble some impressive-looking diagrams and stand next to them looking thoughtful. No one needs to know that's your grocery list disguised as a business strategy.

Action Shots: Bringing Your Daily Grind to Life

Your daily activities are content gold, my friend. You just need to know how to mine it.

1. The Coffee Pour: Nothing says, "I'm a professional with a caffeine addiction," quite like a slow-mo video of you pouring your morning brew.
2. The Power Walk: Film yourself striding purposefully... somewhere. The destination doesn't matter. It is all about the journey (and looking important).
3. The Deep Thought: Capture yourself staring pensively out a window. What are you thinking about? World peace? The meaning of life? Whether you turned off the stove? Your followers will never know.

The Virtual Background Game: Zoom With a View

In the age of virtual everything, your background is your brand. Here is how to level up:

1. The Book Nook: Arrange your most impressive-looking books behind you. Yes, even if you've only read the back covers. Bonus tip: I removed all the glossy covers off my hardback books to help cut down on camera glare and to give it a classier vibe.
2. The Plant Parent: Surround yourself with greenery. It says, "I'm nurturing," and, "I have great air quality," all at once. I have a tall plant placed to create a bit of a frame on the right side of the image that people see of me on their screen. The left side is framed by a bookshelf.
3. The Art Collector: Hang some interesting art behind you. Just make sure it's not so interesting that it distracts from what you say. You also don't want the

image to be so busy that it is difficult to look at the screen for a long time.

Remember, your goal is to look put-together, not like you're broadcasting from the Met.

The Bottom Line: Authenticity With a Filter

At the end of the day, social media is about connection. Yes, we want to look good (thank you, beauty filters), but we also want to be real. Find that sweet spot between polished and authentic, and you'll be swimming in likes. You are not just creating content, you're crafting a visual story of your brand. Make it a page-turner.

That is all the social media wizardry I have for now. Time to put down the phone and step away from the ring light. If anyone needs me, I'll be in the corner, trying to convince Elliott, my eight-pound Norwich Terrier, to be my social media manager. He has great instincts, but his typing skills leave something to be desired. Wish me luck.

MASTERING THE VISUAL LANGUAGE: PUTTING IT ALL TOGETHER

It's time to take all these fabulous pieces you've been juggling and create your masterpiece. Think of it as assembling your own personal Avengers team, but instead of superheroes, you're working with slides, props, attire, social media, and virtual speaking skills. This team-up will be more epic than any movie franchise.

The Art of Visual Harmony: When 1+1=3 (Or Maybe 11, Who's Counting?)

Creating a cohesive visual narrative is like conducting an orchestra. Each element has its part to play, but when they all come together in perfect harmony, that's when the magic happens. Let's break it down:

Slides as the Backbone: Your slides are like the rhythm section of your visual band. They keep the beat, set the tone, and provide a foundation for everything else. But nobody goes to a concert just to see the drummer (sorry, drummers). Your slides should support your narrative, not be the whole show.

Props as the Solo: This is where you get to show off a bit. Like a guitar solo in a rock anthem, your props should be attention-grabbing and memorable, but not so over-the-top that they overshadow everything else.

Attire as the Mood: Your outfit sets the emotional tone, like the key of a song. It should complement your message and your audience, not clash with them.

Unless you're going for a punk rock vibe, in which case, clash away!

Social Media as the Encore: This is where you extend the experience beyond the main event. It is your chance to keep the audience engaged long after the last slide has faded.

Virtual Speaking as the Remix: In the digital world, you don't just perform live—you create a multi-media experience. It is like taking your hit single and adding a sick beat and some autotune (but please, leave the actual autotune to the professionals).

Balancing Act: Too Much of a Good Thing Is... Still Too Much

Before you go full Salvador Dali and throw visual elements around like confetti: balance is key. Create a feast for the eyes, not visual indigestion. Here is how to keep things in check:

The 60-30-10 Rule: In design, this rule suggests using sixty percent of a dominant color, thirty percent of a secondary color, and ten percent of an accent color. Apply this to your visual elements. Let one element (usually your core message) take center stage, support it with secondary elements, and use others for brief moments of emphasis.

The Goldilocks Principle: Not too much, not too little, but just right. If you find yourself saying, "and one more thing," more than Steve Jobs, it might be time to edit.

The Simplicity Paradox: Sometimes, less really is more. As Leonardo da Vinci said, "Simplicity is the ultimate sophistication." Of course, he didn't have to deal with PowerPoint, but the principle still applies.

Adapting Your Visual Symphony: From Carnegie Hall to Instagram Live

Different venues require different approaches. You wouldn't play death metal at a classical music festival (or maybe you would; I don't know your life). Similarly, your visual language needs to adapt to different contexts:

The Big Stage: When you're up on stage, everything needs to be bigger and bolder. Your gestures, your props, your slides—they all need to reach the back row.

The Boardroom: In a more intimate setting, subtlety is your friend. Think fine dining rather than all-you-can-eat buffet.

The Social Media Stage: Here, you're competing with cat videos and dance challenges. Your visuals need to stop the scroll and demand attention at the speed of a viral TikTok.

The Virtual Space: In the land of Zoom, you're not just a speaker—you're a TV producer. Your background, your lighting, your camera angles all become part of your visual language.

The Secret Sauce: Authenticity (With a Side of Pizzazz)

All these elements, all these techniques—they're tools, not rules. The most important thing is that your visual language feels authentic to you. It should be an extension of your personality, your message, your brand.

Think of it like your signature dish. You might follow a recipe at first, but over time, you add your own flair. A dash of this, a pinch of that, and suddenly, it's uniquely yours. Aim for this with your visual language.

The Closing Shot: Your Visual Masterpiece Awaits

Mastering the visual language isn't about becoming the next Wes Anderson (unless that's your goal, in which case, work on your symmetry). It means harnessing the power of visual communication to amplify your message, engage your audience, and leave a lasting impression.

Your challenge? Make a scene. I don't mean the kind where you flip a table in the middle of a board meeting (although, if you do, please send me the video). I am talking about crafting moments so visually compelling, so authentically you, that your audience can't help but be drawn in.

Every great artist started somewhere. Picasso didn't wake up one day and paint Guernica. He practiced, he experimented, he probably made a few weird-looking dogs along the way. Your journey to visual mastery will be the same. Embrace the process, learn from the mishaps, and celebrate the victories.

Throughout this chapter, you've explored the art of visual storytelling—from crafting slides that don't induce narcolepsy to choosing outfits that speak volumes before you utter a word. You have turned props into supporting actors and social media feeds into blockbuster trailers for your personal brand.

Armed with your visual toolkit, go forth and create your masterpiece. Whether it's a presentation that brings the house down, a social media post that breaks the internet, or a virtual meeting that makes people forget they're staring at a screen, you've got this.

Remember, every great director started somewhere. Wes Anderson's first film, *Bottle Rocket*, was a commercial flop. But he kept honing his craft, refining his visual style, and eventually gave us *The Royal Tenenbaums*, *The Grand Budapest Hotel*, and other visual feasts.

Your journey to visual mastery will be similar. There will be mishaps—the PowerPoint that decides to revolt mid-presentation, the prop that refuses to cooperate, the Zoom background that makes you look like you're broadcasting from the moon. Embrace these moments. Learn from them. And then, like any good director, yell, "Take two!" and try again.

And hey, if all else fails, just remember: even the Mona Lisa is just some lady smirking at a painter. Your visual narrative is what you make of it. In the words of *Project Runway*'s Tom Gunn—"Make it work." May the visual force be with you!

We've journeyed through the first four of the Five Stage Languages—Verbal, Vocal, Physical, and Visual. Now it's time to talk about the fifth: The Emotional Language.

** Don't forget to check out:
www.mikeganino.com/bookresources
where I've shared some examples of slides—the notoriously great ones and some infamously not so great ones. **

SET THE SCENE
DETAILS AND IMAGERY
TENSION and RELEASE
PAINT WITH EMOTION

CHAPTER 8

EMOTIONAL LANGUAGE: PAINTING PICTURES IN MINDS AND HEARTS

(OR HOW TO MAKE YOUR AUDIENCE CRY WITHOUT ONIONS OR PUPPIES)

> *"I am a camera, with its shutter open. Someday, all of this will be developed, printed, fixed."*
>
> — **Christopher Isherwood**

THE INVISIBLE PUPPET MASTER

You sit in a dimly lit theater, popcorn in hand, watching the latest blockbuster. Suddenly, your heart starts racing, your palms get sweaty, and you grip the armrest so hard you might leave fingernail marks. Is it because the person next to you decided to open a particularly pungent bag of movie snacks? Nope. It is because the filmmaker has you right where they want you—emotionally hooked, hanging on every frame.

Imagine you could do that with your words. I am not suggesting you become a cinematic supervillain. (Though if that's your dream, who am I to judge?) I am talking about mastering the art of emotional language—the kind that paints vivid pictures in minds and tugs at heartstrings like a virtuoso harpist.

Welcome to the world of emotional puppeteering, where you'll learn to pull the strings of your audience's feelings without them realizing it. We aren't venturing into creepy mind-control territory here. Think of it more as being the conductor of an emotional orchestra, guiding your audience through a symphony of feelings that amplify your message.

You might be thinking, "But Mike, I'm not an evil genius or a master manipulator. I just want people to pay attention during my quarterly sales presentation!" Fear not, my emotionally awkward friend. By the end of this chapter, you'll be serving up emotional connections so powerful, your audience will forget all about checking their phones or planning their next snack run.

I met Anthony Giglio at a winery weekend hosted by friends at Brooks Winery in Oregon. Anthony was there as the guest MC, bringing his larger-than-life personality to the proceedings. Side note: there's a fascinating documentary that includes their story aptly called, "American Wine Story."

For those who don't know Anthony, he's a force of nature in the wine world. An award-winning wine journalist with bylines in *Food & Wine*, *The New Yorker*, and *The Hollywood Reporter*, he's also a media personality who's graced *The Today Show* and *Food Network*. For good measure, he's the Wine Director for The American Express Centurion Global Lounge Network. In short, he knows his grapes.

Over a glass (or three) of Pinot Noir one night, Anthony regaled me with the tale of his Moth story debut. Titled

"Listen Here, Fancy Pants," it's a hilarious romp through his experiences growing up in an Italian American family in New Jersey. But it's not just laughs—Anthony's story is a masterclass in emotional storytelling.

Anthony was a guest on my podcast, The Mike Drop Method, where he broke down the choices he made in telling that story with scenic memories and the emotional beats he wanted to hit. He painted the scene of his childhood home with specific, evocative details—the plastic-covered furniture, the phone hanging on the wall that his mother would rush to answer, the cigarette smoke filling the air as his Grandpa and Dad watched him play with "dolls." There is also a hilarious story about when he asked his Dad, "What's a BJ?" and his Dad's response will have your gut splitting from laughter—yes, I am using a dopamine-inducing hook to get you to go listen to the podcast episode which you can find at:

www.mikeganino.com/anthonygiglio

The title of Anthony's story comes from about three-quarters through this story:

> I remember going home for Sunday supper when I was in my twenties and I was really excited that I had got an assignment to go to Italy to cover a wine event. In an opportunity where Dad should have said, "That's amazing, son," he actually decided to give me a reality check by saying, "Listen here, fancy pants! Don't forget that we know who you are and where you came from and the day you forget it I'll be there to remind you."

That story offered such a level of specificity that you could almost hear the Jersey accent and feel the weight of generational expectations.

But Anthony's storytelling prowess really shines because he doesn't just tell us about the conflict; he makes us feel it. He describes the pit in his stomach as he faces his father, the mixture of pride and guilt as he stands his ground, the love and respect underlying the tension. By the time he reaches the resolution—his father's ultimate support and pride—the audience is fully invested, riding the emotional rollercoaster right alongside him.

I was most struck by Anthony's ability to balance humor and heart. He had the audience in stitches with his descriptions of his *Sopranos*-esque uncles and his mother's plastic-wrapped furniture, but seamlessly transitioned to moments of genuine emotion, like his father's quiet pride at his college graduation.

This, my friends, is the power of emotional language. Anthony didn't just tell us about his experience; he made us feel it. He used specific details, vivid imagery, and carefully crafted moments of tension and release to create an emotional journey for his audience.

Emotions aren't the icing on the cake of communication—they're the whole darn bakery. They make your message stick, and transform forgettable facts into unforgettable experiences. Anthony's story wasn't only about a kid going to college; it was about family, expectations, growth, and love. By tapping into these universal emotions, he created a story that resonated with everyone, regardless of their background.

As we dive deeper into the art of emotional language, keep Anthony's story in mind. Remember how he used specific details to paint a vivid picture, how he balanced humor and heart, and how he created an emotional journey for his audience. These are the tools that will help you transform your own stories from mere recitations of events into powerful, resonant experiences that have your audience asking for buttered popcorn. And just in case you wondered if Anthony and I share opinions on wine, I wholeheartedly agree with this statement he made during our podcast interview: "There is only one wrong answer when it comes to wine—white zinfandel."

So, in the immortal words of Samuel L. Jackson in *Jurassic Park*, "Hold onto your butts." You are about to embark on an emotional roller coaster to make even the most stone-faced audience member feel something. By the time you're done, you'll be painting emotional masterpieces with your words, turning even the driest material into a heart-pounding, tear-jerking, laugh-inducing experience.

Ready to become the Spielberg of storytelling? Let's start pulling those emotional strings. Just remember: with great power comes great responsibility. Use your newfound emotional superpowers for good, not evil. Unless, of course, you're writing a villain's monologue—in which case, go nuts.

THE AUDIENCE'S BRAIN ON STORIES: A CRASH COURSE IN NEUROSCIENCE

Time to put on our mad scientist hats and dive into the squishy, wonderful world of brain chemistry. There won't be a quiz at the end (unless you're into that sort of thing, in which case, we can arrange something).

You see, when you tell a story, you're not just flapping your gums and hoping for the best. You are playing an intricate game of neurochemical Jenga with your audience's brains. And it's a game worth mastering.

Let's break down the fantastic four of storytelling neurotransmitters:

Dopamine: The "Oh Boy, What Happens Next?" Chemical

Dopamine is the overeager puppy of brain chemicals, all about anticipation, reward, and keeping your audience on the edge of their seats. When you trigger dopamine release, you're essentially turning your audience into a bunch of squirrels chasing after the most interesting nut in the world—and that nut is your story.

I have pretty severe ADHD, which is basically a dopamine supply issue. But guess what? It is my superpower when it comes to directing my clients because I'm like a finely tuned boredom detector. If I start zoning out or reaching for my phone, it's a clear sign that we need to up the dopamine ante in their story.

How to Be a Dopamine Dealer (legally, of course):

- Create suspense: “But wait, there’s more!” isn’t just for infomercials.
- Ask questions you’ll answer later: It’s like leaving a trail of storytelling breadcrumbs.
- Use contrast: Mix it up with emotions, pacing, and tone. Be the storytelling equivalent of a mood ring.

But wait, there’s more! (See what I did there?)

Here are some advanced techniques to keep your audience hooked:

- The Cliffhanger Technique: End sections or stories with a tantalizing hint of what’s to come. “And that’s when I realized... the real adventure was just beginning.” Boom. Dopamine hit.
- The Mystery Box: Introduce an intriguing element early on, but don’t reveal its significance until later... like hiding a storytelling Easter egg.
- The Countdown Method: Set up a timeline or deadline within your story. “We had twenty-four hours to save the project...” Tick tock, dopamine clock!
- The Plot Twist: Just when your audience thinks they know where the story is going, pull the rug out from under them... like being a magician, but with words instead of rabbits.

OXYTOCIN: THE "WARM FUZZY FEELINGS" HORMONE

If dopamine is the overeager puppy, oxytocin is the warm, cuddly blanket you wrap yourself in on a cold day, all about empathy, trust, and connection. When you trigger oxytocin, you're not just telling a story—you're making your audience feel part of it.

How to Serve Up Some Oxytocin:

- Get vulnerable: Share those embarrassing, human moments. We have all had toilet paper stuck to our shoe at some point.
- Make it relatable: Find the universal in the specific. Your story about getting lost in a foreign country? That is everyone's story of feeling out of place.

Want to take your oxytocin game to the next level? Try these:

- The "Me Too!" Moment: Share a universal experience or emotion. "Have you ever sent a text to the wrong person and felt your soul leave your body?" Watch the nods of recognition roll in.
- The Underdog Story: People love to root for the little guy. Share stories of overcoming adversity or beating the odds.
- The Gratitude Bomb: Express genuine appreciation for others in your story. It creates a contagious ripple effect of warm fuzzies.
- The Vulnerability Vault: Open up about your fears or insecurities. It is emotional skydiving—scary at first, but exhilarating once you take the leap.

ENDORPHINS: THE "HA! THAT'S FUNNY" HELPERS

Endorphins are the brain's way of saying, "Hey, this is fun!" They are released when we laugh, exercise, or eat chocolate (which explains a lot about my life choices). In storytelling, endorphins are your secret weapon for keeping things light and memorable.

How to Trigger Those Sweet, Sweet Endorphins:

- Sprinkle in some humor: Even serious stories can use a laugh. It is like adding sprinkles to your storytelling sundae.
- Create unexpected twists: Surprise is the spice of storytelling. When they expect you to zig, don't be afraid to zag.

Ready to be an endorphin-releasing machine? Here's how:

- The Call-Back Joke: Reference something funny from earlier in your story. It gives your audience an inside joke to be part of.
- The Self-Deprecating Slice: It is endearing and relatable to poke fun at yourself. "I thought I was having a bad hair day, then I realized... it was my face."
- The Unexpected Comparison: Link two completely unrelated things for comedic effect. "My first attempt at public speaking was like a giraffe on roller skates—awkward, unstable, and people couldn't look away."
- The Physical Comedy Describe: Even in storytelling, a well-described pratfall can be hilarious. Paint a vivid picture of that time you tripped up the stairs (we've all been there).

CORTISOL: THE "OH NO, WHAT'S GOING TO HAPPEN?" HORMONE

Cortisol is the stress hormone, and like that one friend who always brings drama to the party, it needs to be handled with care. A little cortisol can keep your audience engaged, but too much can send them into a full-blown fight-or-flight response. You don't want your audience literally fleeing from your story.

How to Use Cortisol Without Causing a Panic Attack:

- Create tension: Highlight challenges or conflicts, but always provide resolution.
- Use it sparingly: Think of cortisol as the ghost pepper of storytelling. A little goes a long way.

Want to master the art of tension? Try these techniques:

- The Ticking Time Bomb: Introduce a deadline or time constraint. "We had until midnight to submit the proposal, and it was already a quarter to."
- The Near Miss: Describe a close call or narrow escape. It is like a roller coaster—thrilling but safe.
- The Misunderstanding Spiral: Show how a small miscommunication snowballs into bigger problems... anxiety-inducing but fixable.
- The Looming Threat: Hint at a potential danger or challenge on the horizon. This is the storytelling equivalent of ominous background music.

Now, here's where it gets really fun. The true art of storytelling is in mixing these chemicals like a master bartender mixes drinks. You want a neurochemical cocktail that's just right—a little dopamine for anticipation, a splash of oxytocin for connection, a twist of endorphins for fun, and just a dash of cortisol for spice.

The key is balance. You don't want to turn your audience into an emotional yo-yo (unless that's your thing, in which case, yo-yo away). Mix and match these techniques like you're creating a neurochemical smoothie. A dash of dopamine, a sprinkle of oxytocin, a handful of endorphins, and just a pinch of cortisol. Blend well, serve chilled, and watch as your audience drinks it all in.

Remember, with great power comes great responsibility. Use your newfound neuroscience knowledge for good, not evil. Unless, of course, you really are writing a villain's monologue, in which case, go full mad scientist. Just don't blame me if your audience starts gathering torches and pitchforks.

Now, who's ready to play some neurochemical Jenga? Go forth and be the brain chemist you were always meant to be, and concoct really engaging stories.

PULLING THE EMOTIONAL STRINGS: TECHNIQUES FOR EMOTIONAL CONTROL

Alright, storytelling puppeteers, it's time to learn how to pull those heartstrings without getting tangled up in your own narrative threads. This is the art of emotional control—or as I like to call it, "How to Make Your Audience Feel Things Without Resorting to Onions or Puppies."

You are not here to manipulate emotions like storytelling supervillains but to create genuine connections and impactful narratives. Put on your emotional conductor hat (it's invisible but very stylish), and let's get started!

THE DOPAMINE SUPERPOWER: GETTING THEM HOOKED

Dopamine is the superpower of communication, the "I gotta know what happens next!" chemical. The best way to trigger it? Get your audience to anticipate a reward. Make them curious. How? By raising the stakes and giving them a reason to listen.

The "I Want Song" Technique

This isn't about bursting into a musical number (although, if that's your thing, sing your heart out). The "I Want Song" is a concept from musicals—think "Part of Your World" from *The Little Mermaid* or "My Shot" from *Hamilton*. It is a clear statement of desire that sets the stage for everything that follows.

Your story or message needs an "I Want Song" moment right at the beginning, putting up a big neon sign that says, "Here's where we're going, folks!" It gets your audience immediately into the scene and invested in the outcome.

The Inner Monologue: Welcome to My Brain

If I could give every storyteller one tool, it would be the inner monologue. This is where you crack open your skull (figuratively, please) and let the audience peek inside. Share your thoughts, fears, hopes, and dreams. Let them into your mind.

For example, as you recount a moment of decision, describe what races through your mind: "As my hand hovered over the 'Send' button, a thousand thoughts raced through my mind. What if this email ruined my career? What if it saved it? What if I'd accidentally attached that embarrassing cat meme instead of the quarterly report?"

This builds tension and makes the audience feel the gravity of the situation, giving them a backstage pass to your brain.

The Basecamp Moment: Packing for the Emotional Journey

Picture a group of hikers at basecamp, checking their gear before tackling Everest. The Basecamp Moment is when you lay out all the emotional equipment—your aspirations, your fears, what's at stake—before a crucial moment in your story.

"Before I walked into that interview, I took a deep breath. This wasn't just a job—it was proving to myself that taking that risk, quitting my safe but soul-crushing corporate gig, and pursuing my passion wasn't a colossal mistake. My entire future hinged on the next thirty minutes."

By doing this, you're not just telling a story—you're strapping your audience into an emotional roller coaster and daring them not to scream.

The Prophecy: The Art of the False Prediction

This technique is like being a storytelling fortune teller, but with a twist. You make a prediction within your story, often about an impending outcome. The audience starts to anticipate it, but—plot twist! —it doesn't come true.

"I saw her number on my phone. I knew it was the manager from the interview, calling to tell me they'd picked another candidate. My decision to rawdog a story about an Argentinian winemaker had backfired, and now I wouldn't get the dream job. I took a breath, considered tossing my phone into Lake Michigan, and then answered."

This keeps the audience on edge, wondering if the prediction will come true, like narrative bungee jumping—the thrill is in the anticipation of the fall.

The Zach Morris Freeze: Time Out for Feels

Remember Zach Morris from *Saved by the Bell* when he froze the scene and talked directly to the audience? You can do the same in your storytelling (minus the nineties haircut).

Use this to slow down a moment, dive deeper into your thoughts, or tease the audience about what's coming next. "And there I was, about to press 'send' on the email that would change everything. But before we get to that, let me tell you about the series of questionable decisions that led me to this moment..."

The Law and Order Clue: Hide in Plain Sight

In *Law and Order*, they often leave obvious clues just hanging out, waiting for someone to notice. You can do the same in your story. Drop subtle hints or details that will pay off later, leaving a trail of narrative breadcrumbs for your audience to follow.

SUSPENSE: THE ART OF "WHAT HAPPENS NEXT?"

Suspense is all about creating that delicious anxiety in your audience, including enough information to get them hooked, but leaving out juuuust enough to keep them on the edge of their seats.

My client Dana V. Adams was working with me on a ten-minute story she'd be telling at The Failure Ball—a 501(c)(3) nonprofit that raises money for suicide prevention by throwing a fancy ball where select storytellers stand up to give a toast to failure with a personal story. I happen to be on the board of the event. Dana started with a very chronological retelling of a relationship failure—or rather her failure in recognizing the red flags in a relationship.

We decided to start the story like this:

> I open the Facebook direct message from my friend and see a link to a podcast. It's a link for a podcast, but I've never heard it before. I see it's about Him and I think *Oh My Gosh*, it's finally caught up with him! It's hard to believe that was eighteen years ago. It was an evening similar to tonight ...

She goes on to tell the story of the start of that relationship. It isn't until the end of the story that we revisit the scene with the Facebook message. In that final scene, she reveals the big secret of what exactly "caught up with him." Throughout the story, she keeps weaving surprise and intrigue, too, but right from the start she has the audience in the palm of her hand ready to find out what happened. And you really should have been at The Failure Ball to hear it for yourself. It is her story to tell, not mine. But she delivered a great message that night.

The "Breadcrumb Trail" Technique

Leave a trail of clues or hints throughout your story, each building anticipation for the big reveal.

Pro Tip: Think of it like setting up a surprise party for your audience. Each hint is a balloon or streamer they glimpse before the big "*surprise!*"

The "What's in the Box?" Technique

Introduce a mystery element early on, but delay the reveal. This is the storytelling equivalent of that unopened present under the Christmas tree. Example: "The small black box sat on my desk all day. It wasn't until five pm that I finally learned its contents... and nothing would ever be the same."

The "Almost, But Not Quite" Method

Bring your audience to the brink of a resolution, then pull back at the last second. It is like narrative edging (keep it clean, folks). Example: "I reached for the door handle, ready to confront my boss. My fingers were just about to touch the cool metal when suddenly..."

Surprise! The Power of the Unexpected

The "Plot Twist Pretzel" Method

Just when your audience thinks they know where the story is going, throw them for a loop. It is like being a narrative chiropractor—you're here to adjust their expectations. Example: "After weeks of suspecting my coworker of stealing office supplies, I finally caught the real culprit red-handed. Plot twist: it was the CEO's therapy llama." (Yes, therapy llamas are a thing. Look it up.)

The "Expectation Subversion" Technique

Set up a common scenario, then flip it on its head, the storytelling equivalent of a jack-in-the-box. Example: "I braced myself for the worst performance review of my life. Instead, my boss handed me a promotion and a basket of muffins."

HUMOR WITHOUT THE BA-DUM-TSS

Surprise is why humor works on stage—without having to resort to lame jokes. It is all about subverting expectations. Set up a scenario that seems to be going one way, then take a sharp left into Unexpected-ville.

For example: "I decided to take up meditation to reduce stress. Two weeks later, I was more relaxed than ever... and accidentally joined a cult. Turns out, always saying 'yes' to your meditation teacher has its downsides."

The key is to lead your audience down one path, then suddenly reveal you're on a completely different road, like being a comedic GPS: "Recalculating route to punchline!"

TENSE AND PERSPECTIVE: CHOOSING YOUR EMOTIONAL LENS

The Time-Hopping Narrator

Switch between past and present tense to create emotional contrast and build anticipation. Example: "I walk into the conference room, palms sweating. But let me back up and tell you how I got here..."

The Unreliable Narrator

Tell the story from a biased or limited perspective, then reveal the truth later, playing emotional peek-a-boo with your audience. Example: "I was certain Janet from Accounting was out to get me. Turns out, she was planning my surprise birthday party all along. Oops."

The Fly on the Wall

Narrate events as if you're an omniscient observer, like giving your audience a storytelling God mode. Example: "Little did John know, as he microwaved his sad desk lunch, that in just thirty-seven minutes, his life would change forever..."

HOW WE KILL THE BUZZ: THE DON'TS OF EMOTIONAL STORYTELLING

Now we've covered how to create emotional buzz, let's talk about how we often accidentally murder it in cold blood. Here are some common buzz-killers:

1. The Spoiler Alert: Not recognizing where the moment of surprise was in your actual experience, so you fail to recreate the moment of surprise in your retelling. We often communicate with hindsight—but we didn't have that at the time. Don't rob your audience of the surprise you felt.
2. The Premature Lede: Putting a summary where an "I Want Song" belongs. "This is a story about how four simple words from my toddler helped me see I was a good dad." Congratulations, you've just killed all suspense, stakes, and surprise. Why should anyone listen now?
3. The Emotional Signpost: Indicating emotions instead of creating them. "And you will never believe how I found out," or, "The road to profit was definitely paved with trouble." These are just loud signposts telling the audience what they're supposed to feel, instead of, you know, actually making them feel those things.
4. The Storytelling Spoiler: Prefacing your story with its moral or outcome. "Let me tell you how I learned that treating your customers well from the start is the most important lesson in business." Great, now we can all go home, right?

Make your audience feel like they're discovering the story alongside you, not being handed a pre-digested moral. Keep the mystery alive, folks!

My client, Shelley Paxton, has a story in her keynote about this moment when she has a recurring nightmare and finally decides to leave her job at Harley Davidson. In the original version, she started with that fact—and then talked to the audience about how often we feel this way and shared stats and data about burnout, workplace success, and personal stress. Once she had made that point, she finally told us about the recurring nightmare that pushed her into leaving, writing her book, and becoming a keynote speaker.

It was fine. It was energetic. But it lacked the level of emotional connection that an experience of that caliber deserves.

We rewrote it so that she walks on stage and immediately says, "I'm watching my team celebrate at one of those NYC restaurants where you take your team to celebrate. We're cheers-ing, ordering more bottles of wine, and celebrating our win. We've just launched..." and she goes into the product they'd just launched which was covered in *Time Magazine*. She puts us right into the scene. She talks about starting to feel anxious again as the night winds down because she realizes she will have to go back to her room alone.

The audience wonders what is happening, why this successful person has this feeling, and what is she scared of in her room. She talks about being in the elevator and considering what other options she has besides going to her room, until she does go in and repeats to herself, "It's not going to happen again tonight," until she falls asleep. Then: "I'm standing in a dark corridor." She goes into the nightmare scene.

This story is now one that instantly grabs the audience's attention, hijacks their dopamine response, and gets them emotionally invested in the experience she is sharing with them.

So there you have it, my emotional architects. You are now armed with the tools to build some narrative skyscrapers that touch the hearts of your audience. Just remember to install some emotional elevators—nobody likes to be stuck at the top of Feelings Mountain without a way down.

And hey, if all else fails, you can always fall back on the ultimate emotional technique: pictures of baby animals. But save that for emergencies only.

MIND MOVIES: CREATING VIVID MENTAL IMAGES

Aspiring Spielbergs of the spoken word, let's talk about how to turn your audience's minds into IMAX theaters. Not actual mind control (though if you figure that out, call me) but the art of creating vivid mental images that make your stories pop like a 3D movie—without the annoying glasses.

The Spoken Word Challenge: No Props, No Problem

Unlike movies, plays, or TV shows, we don't have the luxury of sets, costumes, or Ryan Gosling's abs to help tell our story. And unlike novels, our audience can't flip back a few pages when they zone out thinking about what to have for dinner.

Nope, in the world of spoken storytelling, we're working without a net. If our audience stops to ponder the deeper meaning of life for a second, they miss whatever brilliant thing we said. Our job is to keep them with us, painting pictures with our words faster than Bob Ross on espresso.

Setting the Scene: Give Them Somewhere to Stand

First things first, give a physical location as close to the beginning of your story as possible. It is like giving your audience a mental green screen to project your story onto.

"I was standing in line at the DMV," immediately puts your audience in a familiar (and probably slightly depressing) setting. They can smell the stale air, feel the hard plastic chairs, hear the monotonous, "Now serving number 273," announcement.

If you don't keep them in a location, you've left Storytelling Land and entered Lecture and Essay Valley. Nobody wants to vacation there. If you're going to "make a scene" (see what I did there?), you need a place for the scene to happen. Otherwise, it's just you flailing your arms in an empty void. Save that for your interpretive dance phase.

The Art of Description: Paint With Emotion, Not Wikipedia

Now, let's talk about how to describe things in a way that doesn't put your audience to sleep faster than a documentary on the history of beige paint.

> **Bad example:**
>
> "She was so much prettier than me at 5'9" with blonde hair, blue eyes, perfectly tanned skin, and white teeth."

Congratulations, you've just described half the population of Southern California and bored your audience to tears.

> **Good example:**
>
> "We smiled at each other and walked into the party. And it happened again—I immediately became

invisible to everyone in the room. She had the kind of look that just magnetized everyone's attention to her. I imagined even Marilyn Monroe feeling small next to her. I wanted to hate her for her perfect everything—but she was also the first person to grab my hand and walk me into the middle of every party she was ever invited to. That's Lori."

See the difference? The second example doesn't just describe Lori—it makes us feel something about her. It paints a picture of her impact, not just her appearance. It is the difference between a police sketch and a Rembrandt.

The Sensory Sweet Spot: Goldilocks Would Approve

When it comes to sensory detail, aim for the Goldilocks zone: not too much, not too little, but juuuust right.

Too little, and your audience floats in a void. Too much, and they drown in a sea of adjectives, desperately grasping for the life raft of your actual point.

You aren't writing the next great American novel here. You aren't trying to make them imagine the exact shade of blue on the wall (unless that blue is crucial to your story—like if you're talking about how you accidentally painted your entire house Smurf blue).

We want them to connect emotionally, not feel like they're taking a virtual reality tour of your memory. Unless you plan to sell tickets to your mental theme park, in which case, ignore everything I just said and describe every dust mote in excruciating detail.

The Wikipedia Trap: Don't Fall In

A common pitfall is that of turning your story into a Wikipedia page. "The coffee shop, established in 1998, was located at the corner of Fifth and Main, and served an average of five hundred customers per day..."

Yawn. Unless your story is about how you uncovered a massive coffee shop conspiracy (in which case, I'm all ears), we don't need the full history and stats.

Instead, give us the details that matter emotionally. "The coffee shop was my second home—the kind of place where the barista starts making your usual before you even reach the counter, and where the worn leather armchair in the corner feels like it was molded specifically for your butt."

My client, Tiffany Lanier, has a story about her favorite brunch food—chilaquiles. A restaurant took them off their menu, which she discovered when she excitedly attempted to order them on her birthday. Originally the story started with a prologue about how much she loved chilaquiles and always looked forward to eating them, then moved into her traveling to the restaurant and entering the front door. A fine story—but lots of information before we ever get to something happening.

We workshopped the story so that it starts at the moment the server comes to the table and asks if they want to hear the specials. Tiffany responds that she doesn't need to because she already knows what she wants—then does a little backstory on this being her favorite place for her favorite birthday meal. When she says she will have the chilaquiles with green sauce ***and*** a fried egg on top, the server tells her they took it off the menu.

From there Tiffany goes into some inner monologue about how thrown off it made her and how upset she got before finally turning the story toward the insight she shares with her audience. You'll have to book her for a keynote to hear the rest.

By starting in the moment when something happened (ordering her favorite dish), Tiffany gets us right into the story, right into the predicament, and hooked to hear what happens next.

Action Item: Make a Scene, Not a Lecture

So, here's your mission, should you choose to accept it (and if you've read this far, you're kind of committed now):

1. Set the scene early. Give your audience a place to stand in your story.
2. Paint with emotion, not facts. Make them feel, not just see.
3. Find the sensory sweet spot. Enough to immerse, not enough to drown.
4. Avoid the Wikipedia trap. You're a storyteller, not Alexa.

Remember, your goal is to create a mind movie so vivid, your audience forgets they're listening to you and starts reaching for the popcorn.

Now go forth and paint those mental masterpieces. Just try not to give anyone motion sickness with your vivid descriptions of rollercoaster rides. I don't want to be held responsible for any dry-cleaning bills.

CONCLUSION: PAINTING EMOTIONAL MASTERPIECES

Well, storytelling Picassos, you've reached the end of your crash course in emotional alchemy. You have learned how to turn boring anecdotes into edge-of-your-seat thrillers, how to make your audience laugh, cry, and possibly question their life choices—all with the power of your words.

Let's recap your journey through the emotional landscape:

1. We dove into the squishy world of brain chemistry, learning how to cocktail those neurotransmitters like a master bartender at the Storytelling Speakeasy.
2. We explored techniques to pull those emotional strings without tangling ourselves up in them. Remember, you're aiming for "master puppeteer," not "kid playing with spaghetti."
3. We learned how to create mind movies so vivid, your audience might start reaching for 3D glasses. With great power comes great responsibility—use your descriptive powers for good, not evil (or at least not for boring people to tears).

Your goal isn't to manipulate emotions like some kind of storytelling supervillain. Create genuine connections, make your message stick, and possibly make people snort-laugh in public places. Use your newfound powers wisely, and maybe keep some tissues handy—you never know when you might accidentally inspire a tearjerker moment.

But here's the thing: all this knowledge is as useful as a chocolate teapot if you don't put it into practice. Your mission, should you choose to accept it (and let's face it, you're in too deep to back out now), is to go forth and make some emotional scenes.

Start small. Maybe make the barista at your local coffee shop tear up a little when you describe your desperate need for caffeine. Work your way up to moving your entire office to standing ovations with your quarterly sales reports. The emotional world is your oyster—go shuck it! (Sorry, that was shellfish of me.)

As you move into Part 3, where you'll put all these pieces together, keep this in mind: Every story you tell is a chance to paint an emotional masterpiece. So grab your word-brush, dip it in some feelings, and start creating your narrative Mona Lisa.

And hey, if all else fails, fall back on pictures of baby animals. But let's consider that the nuclear option of emotional storytelling, shall we?

ACT 3

THINK LIKE A DIRECTOR

(OR HOW TO BECOME THE SPIELBERG OF YOUR OWN LIFE STORY)

"When you're telling a story, you're using the entirety of your craft, of your technical prowess, to emotionally engage an audience."

– Joe Russo, Director – Avengers: Endgame; Arrested Development

Let's shatter another myth: Rehearsal is not the holy grail of great performances. *Gasp!* I know, I know. It is like I just told you Santa isn't real. Now that you have explored the Five Stage Languages and how to expand the range of what's possible for you (and how those things impact your audience), it's time to put them all together as you start to workshop and prep for your moment.

Traditional rehearsal methods are about as exciting as watching paint dry, and about as effective as trying to nail Jell-O to a wall. They turn vibrant, living stories into robotic recitations.

You're at a conference, and the speaker takes the stage. They start their talk, and it's... fine. The words are right, the slides are pretty, but something's missing. It is like watching a very well-trained parrot recite Shakespeare. Technically impressive, but where's the soul?

That, my friends, is the result of over-rehearsal and memorization, the reason so many talks feel as alive as that ficus plant in the corner of your office. (You know, the one you keep forgetting to water?)

I once had a storytelling attendee who froze mid-competition because she couldn't remember the next memorized line. It was like watching a computer crash in real time. Blue screen of death and all. Not pretty.

So, what's the alternative? I am glad you asked. Welcome to the world of Rapid Prototyping.

Think of it this way: Did *Hamilton* spring fully formed from Lin-Manuel Miranda's mind like Athena from Zeus's forehead? (Mythology reference. Boom! We're getting cultured here.) Of course not! It was refined through years of workshopping, countless revisions, performances, and feedback loops.

You need to do the same. Treat your material like a living, breathing entity. Explore it, play with it, tweak it, and perfect it. Make it so familiar to you that you could deliver it in your sleep (though sleeping through your presentations is generally frowned upon).

This section dives into the Five-Step Rapid Prototyping Process:

1. Read It: Break down your script and find the emotional beats.
2. Improv It (with notes): Start playing and integrating those Five Stage Languages.
3. Improv It (no notes): Where the magic happens. You're going off-book, baby!
4. Run It: Full dress rehearsal time. Lights, camera, action!
5. Work It: Refine, refine, refine. Like a fine wine, your performance gets better with time.

Pro tip: At no point in this process will you sit and stare at slides, trying to burn them onto your retinas. That isn't preparation; that's self-inflicted torture. You will be active, dynamic, and dare I say it, actually having fun while you prepare.

By the end of this section, you'll know how to workshop your material like a Broadway pro, how to give and receive feedback that actually helps (no more "um, that was... nice" comments), and how to polish your performance until it shines brighter than a disco ball at Studio 54. (Google it, kids.)

You will learn to trust the process, embrace imperfection, and be present in the moment. When you step on that stage, you're not just delivering information—you're creating an experience. Making a *scene*. And it's going to be spectacular.

So, are you ready to ditch the robotic rehearsals and embrace your inner improv star? Let's dive in and start making some scenes!

YES!
1
2
3
4
5
AND!

CHAPTER 9

THE RAPID PROTOTYPING PROTOCOL

(OR THE "YES, AND" APPROACH TO NAILING YOUR NEXT PRESENTATION)

> *"Luck? I don't know anything about luck. I've never banked on it, and I'm afraid of people who do. Luck to me is something else: hard work—and realizing what opportunity is and what isn't."*
>
> **— Lucille Ball**

You're backstage, palms sweaty, knees weak, arms are heavy (thanks, Eminem). You have spent weeks rehearsing your presentation, memorizing every word, every pause, every gesture. You step out onto the stage, take a deep breath, and... blank. Your mind goes as empty as a politician's promises. Suddenly, you're not a polished presenter—you're a deer in headlights, praying for the sweet release of a trap door opening beneath your feet.

Sound familiar? If you've ever suffered through the special hell that is over-rehearsing, you're not alone. But what if I told you there was a better way? A way to prepare that doesn't involve turning yourself into a very anxious robot? Enter: Rapid Prototyping.

I know you're thinking, "Mike, that sounds like something from a Silicon Valley startup, not a communication technique." And you're not entirely wrong. But just like how peanut butter and jelly found their soulmates in each other, the world of tech and the art of storytelling have created magic together.

Rapid Prototyping is my love child of improv comedy and the iterative design process we would use to devise new scripted shows and sketch comedy routines. When I first started directing speakers, I need to come up with a repeatable process for them to follow for their keynotes, presentations, and media opportunities. I knew it had to also avoid them memorizing their scripts in a way that usually ends up with the speaker sounded like a Victorian era aristocrat devoid all of all the spice and energy of their communication style. The method allows you to workshop your material like a Broadway pro, refine your delivery like a stand-up comedian, and connect with your audience like a seasoned talk show host. All this, without the mind-numbing repetition that makes traditional rehearsal feel like *Groundhog Day*, minus the charm of Bill Murray.

This chapter breaks down the Rapid Prototyping process, showing you how to turn your presentations from robotic recitations into living, breathing performances. You will explore each step of the process, from "Read It" to "Work It" and find the tools to make your material so familiar, you could deliver it in your sleep.

You are about to turn rehearsal on its head and make preparation not just effective, but dare I say it... fun. Let's dive deeper into what Rapid Prototyping is and why it's the secret sauce to killer presentations.

WHAT THE HECK IS RAPID PROTOTYPING ANYWAY?

Rapid Prototyping is the cool, creative cousin of traditional rehearsal. It takes the best parts of improv comedy, iterative design, and good old-fashioned playfulness, and mashes them together into a preparation technique that's enjoyable. I know, enjoyable preparation—sounds like an oxymoron, right? But stick with me here.

In essence, Rapid Prototyping is about creating multiple "prototypes" or versions of your presentation quickly, rather than trying to perfect one version through endless repetition. It is like speed dating for your content—you get to try out different approaches, see what clicks, and refine based on what works best.

Here is why it's a game-changer:

1. It Keeps Things Fresh: Unlike traditional rehearsal, which can leave you sounding like a well-programmed Alexa, Rapid Prototyping keeps your delivery spontaneous and alive. You aren't memorizing lines; you're internalizing concepts.
2. It Is Failure-Friendly: In the world of Rapid Prototyping, there's no such thing as a mistake—only happy accidents. (Bob Ross would be proud.) Each "failure" is just data that helps you improve the next iteration.
3. It Is Efficient: Instead of spending hours perfecting one way of saying something, you can quickly test multiple approaches and find the one that resonates most.
4. It Is Adaptable: Life is unpredictable, and so are presentations. Rapid Prototyping makes you nimble enough to handle whatever curveballs come your way.

Forgot a line? No problem. You know the concept inside and out.

5. It Is Fun: I know, I know. "Fun" and "presentation prep" in the same sentence feels wrong. But once you start playing with your content instead of just reciting it, you'll wonder why you ever did it any other way.

I hear some of you skeptics out there. "But Mike," you say, "I'm not a comedian or a tech guru. How can this possibly work for me?"

Well, my doubting friend, let me tell you a little story. I once worked with a client—let's call her Jessica—who was the human embodiment of stage fright. Her idea of preparation was writing out her entire speech word for word and then reading it aloud to her corgi approximately 7,492 times. (The corgi, by the way, was not impressed.)

When I introduced her to Rapid Prototyping, she looked at me like I'd suggested she deliver her next board presentation while juggling flaming torches. But once we got started, something magical happened. She started to have fun. She played with different ways of telling her story. She made mistakes and laughed them off. And when it came time for the real presentation? She nailed it. Not because she had memorized every word, but because she knew her content so well, she could roll with whatever came her way.

That is the power of Rapid Prototyping. It turns preparation from a chore into a chance to play, explore, and truly own your material. And the best part? You don't need any special skills or equipment. Just your content, your creativity, and a willingness to embrace a little controlled chaos.

THE FIVE-STEP RAPID PROTOTYPING PROCESS: YOUR ROADMAP TO PRESENTATION PERFECTION

It is time to break down the Rapid Prototyping process. Think of these five steps as your yellow brick road to Oz, except instead of meeting a wizard, you're becoming one. A wizard of words, that is. So, grab your metaphorical hard hat because you're about to construct one heck of a presentation.

Step 1: Read It —Becoming the Morgan Freeman of Your Own Story

First things first, get intimate with your material. I don't mean taking your script out for a candlelit dinner (although, hey, whatever works for you). This step is all about reading your content aloud, like you're the world's most engaging audiobook narrator. Channel your inner Morgan Freeman, people!

This is the key: don't just read it: feel it. Notice where the energy peaks and valleys are. Where does your voice naturally get excited? Where does it slow down? These are your emotional beats, and they're gold dust for your presentation.

> **Pro Tip:** Record yourself during this step. Yes, I know hearing your own voice is about as pleasant as nails on a chalkboard. But you'll pick up on things you never noticed before. Plus, it's great material for your future biopic.

Why It Matters:

Reading aloud does more than familiarize you with your content. It is like taking your words out for a test drive. You can hear how they sound, feel how they flow, and notice where you stumble (hopefully not as dramatically as I did during my first TED talk when I practically tripped over my own tongue).

How to Do It:

1. Find a quiet space. Your shower works great, plus the acoustics are amazing. Just don't drop your script—wet paper is nobody's friend.
2. Read with feeling. If you're talking about your company's record-breaking quarter, sound excited! If you're discussing a challenging problem, let that concern creep into your voice. Basically, emote like you're auditioning for a soap opera.
3. Pay attention to your natural pauses and emphases. Where do you naturally speed up or slow down? These are clues to the rhythm of your speech.
4. Record yourself. It is invaluable. Plus, you might discover a hidden talent for voice acting. Next stop, Pixar!

Action:

The "Ridiculous Renditions" Exercise: Read your content in three totally different ways. Try it as a news anchor, then as a passionate preacher, and finally as a conspiratorial whisper. It sounds silly (and it is), but it'll help you find new dimensions in your delivery.

Real-Life Example:

I once had a client, let's call him Bob, who was preparing for a big product launch. His initial read-through was flatter than a pancake run over by a steamroller. I had him read it as if he was a ringmaster introducing the greatest show on earth. Suddenly, his energy skyrocketed, his pacing improved, and he found the excitement in his own words. The actual presentation? He knocked it out of the park. No circus tent required.

Step 2: Improv It (with notes) —Embracing Your Inner Yes-And

Welcome to the "Improv It (with notes)" phase, or as I like to call it, "Controlled Chaos 101." This is where we loosen up and play with our content. Think of your notes as the bumpers on a bowling lane—there to keep you on track, but the real fun happens in between.

Start riffing on your material. Try telling your story in different ways. What happens if you start at the end? What if you tell it from a different perspective? This is your chance to channel your inner Robin Williams (rest in peace, you beautiful, hilarious soul).

There are no mistakes here, only happy accidents. If you go off on a tangent about your cat's weird obsession with your laptop charger, go with it. You never know, it might end up being comedy gold.

Why It Matters:

Improvising with your notes helps you internalize your content in a way that rigid memorization never could. It is the difference between knowing the words and understanding the music. Plus, it's a lot more fun than staring at your script until your eyes bleed.

How to Do It:

1. Start with your main points as guideposts. These are your safe harbors in the sea of improvisation.
2. Riff on each point. If you were explaining this to your best friend over coffee, what examples would you use? What analogies might come to mind?
3. Don't be afraid to go off on tangents. Sometimes the scenic route leads to the best destinations.
4. Embrace the "Yes, And" principle from improv comedy. Whatever idea comes to mind, run with it and see where it goes.

Action:

The "Random Word" Challenge: Have a friend give you a random word for each main point in your presentation. Your job is to connect that word to your content somehow. It is like mental gymnastics, but with less risk of pulling a hamstring.

Real-Life Example:

I once worked with a CFO who was about as exciting as watching paint dry in slow motion. His quarterly reports were pure NyQuil. So, we played the Random Word game. He got "banana" for the section on profit margins. Suddenly, he was comparing profit margins to the layers of a banana, with the peel representing overhead costs. Was it a bit weird? Sure. But it was memorable, understandable, and dare I say, a-peel-ing. (Sorry, not sorry.)

Step 3: Improv It (no notes)—Flying Without a Net

Welcome to the "Improv It (no notes)" phase, aka "The Freestyle Olympics." In this step, ditch the notes entirely. I know, I know—it's scarier than that time you accidentally liked your ex's Instagram post from 2015. But it's not as terrifying as it seems.

Your goal isn't to recite your content word-for-word. It is to play with the core ideas and see where they take you. You might find new angles you never considered before. You might discover a killer opening line. You might also ramble about your weird dream from last night for five minutes. It is all part of the process.

Why It Matters:

This step is about developing a deep, intuitive understanding of your material. When you can riff on your content without notes, you're no longer reciting—you're conversing. It is the difference between reading a map and knowing the terrain by heart.

Pro Tip: This is a great time to rope in a friend or colleague as your audience. Their reactions can give you valuable feedback. Plus, it's always fun to have someone witness your periodic moments of genius (and occasional moments of, "What the heck was that?").

How to Do It:

1. Start with your opening line, then just... go. Let your stream of consciousness take over.
2. Don't worry about getting everything "right." The goal is flow, not perfection.
3. If you get stuck, don't panic. Take a breath, recap where you've been, and let that guide you to where you're going.
4. Embrace tangents. Sometimes they lead nowhere, but sometimes they lead to storytelling gold.

Action:

The "Presentation Roulette" Game: Write each main point of your presentation on a separate piece of paper. Throw them up in the air and pick them up in random order. Now, give your presentation in that order. It is like Presentation Twister, but with less risk of pulling a muscle.

Real-Life Example:

I had a client, let's call him Aaron, who was petrified of speaking without notes. So, we played Presentation Roulette. At first, he was a deer in headlights. But as she kept going, something magical happened. He started making connections between his points that he'd never seen before. He found new ways to transition. By the end, he wasn't just reciting information, he was weaving a story. And when it came time for his actual presentation? Aaron rocked it, no notes required.

Your goal isn't to create a perfect, word-for-word recitation, but to become so comfortable with your material that you could discuss it as easily as you'd chat about your favorite TV show. (And if your favorite show happens to be about quarterly earnings reports, well, you might be in the wrong line of work.)

Step 4: Run It—Lights, Camera, Action!

Welcome to the "Run It" phase, or as I like to call it, "Dress Rehearsal on Steroids." This is where you take everything you've been playing with and put it all together, like assembling a Voltron of presentation skills. (If you don't get that reference, ask your nearest eighties kid.) This is where you do a full run-through, as if you're giving the real presentation.

Set the stage as much as possible. If you'll be standing for your actual presentation, stand now. If you have slides, use them. Heck, if you will be presenting in a chicken suit (hey, I don't know your life), put that bad boy on. True story: I have on three separate occasions given a keynote wearing a taco costume.

The key is to make it as real as possible. This helps your brain associate the physical act of presenting with the content you've been playing with, like Pavlov's dogs, but instead of drooling at a bell, you nail your presentation at the sight of a podium.

Why It Matters:

This step is as close as you'll get to the real deal without actually being there. It is your chance to iron out any kinks, identify any weak spots, and get a feel for the flow of your entire presentation. Plus, it's a great excuse to wear your power suit around the house.

How to Do It:

1. Set the stage: Recreate your presentation environment as much as possible. If you'll be standing behind a podium, set one up (a stack of boxes works in a pinch). If you'll be using slides, use them now.
2. Dress the part: Wear what you'll wear on the day. Yes, even if that means donning a full suit to present to your cat. (Trust me, Mr. Whiskers is a tough audience.)

3. Use your props: If you plan to use props or visual aids, incorporate them now. This is your chance to make sure that brilliant visual metaphor doesn't turn into a brilliant disaster.
4. Time yourself: Know your time constraints and stick to them. Nothing says, "I don't respect your time," quite like a presentation that runs longer than the director's cut of *Lord of the Rings*.

Action:

The "Worst Case Scenario" Drill: Run through your presentation, but have a friend randomly interject with potential disasters. Your slides won't load. The mic cuts out. A meteor is headed for Earth. Okay, maybe not that last one, but you get the idea. The point is to practice adapting on the fly.

Real-Life Example:

I once worked with a tech CEO preparing for a major product launch. During our "Run It" phase, I had his team act as the audience, peppering him with tough questions and even heckling a bit. (I may have enjoyed that part a little too much.) At first, he was rattled. But as we kept at it, he got more and more comfortable handling unexpected situations. When the real launch came around, he was cool as a cucumber, even when faced with some pretty aggressive questioning from the press. He later told me it felt easy compared to our practice sessions. Mission accomplished!

Step 5: Work It—Polish Until It Shines

Welcome to the final step, the "Work It" phase. This is where we take your presentation from "pretty good" to "holy cow, did you see that?" It is like giving your content a spa day, complete with a facial, mani-pedi, and a seaweed wrap. (Your words will thank you, trust me.)

Maybe you realized that your opening needs more punch. Perhaps you discovered a killer analogy during your improv sessions. Or maybe you found out that your chicken suit is really, really itchy and you need to rethink your wardrobe choices.

Whatever insights you've gained, now is the time to incorporate them. But remember, you're not aiming for word-perfect memorization here. Aim for a deep, internalized understanding of your content that allows you to be flexible and natural in your delivery.

Why It Matters:

This step is all about refinement. You take all the insights from the previous steps and use them to elevate your presentation. Think of it as fine-tuning your instrument before the big concert.

How to Do It:

1. Reflect on your run-throughs: What worked well? What felt clunky? Where did you consistently stumble?
2. Solicit feedback: If you had an audience for your run-through, get their input. What resonated with them? What confused them? What made them check their watch?
3. Tighten your language: Look for places where you can say more with less. As Mark Twain said, "I didn't

have time to write a short letter, so I wrote a long one instead." Make time for that short letter.

4. Amp up your openings and closings: These are prime real estate in your presentation. Make sure they pack a punch.
5. Refine your delivery: Work on your pacing, your emphasis, your gestures. But go for natural and authentic, not, "robot trying to impersonate a human." Use your experience in the previous parts of the Rapid Prototyping Protocol to continue to set new goals and reach for new heights. Never walk into a presentation without a *Five Stage Language* related goal.

Action:

The "Explain It to a Kid" Challenge: Try explaining your key points to a child (real or imaginary). If you can make a ten-year-old understand and care about your quarterly earnings report, you're on the right track.

Real-Life Example:

I once worked with a brilliant scientist preparing a TED talk on climate change. Her content was solid, but it was drier than the Sahara in a drought. During our "Work It" phase, we focused on finding analogies that would resonate with a general audience. We ended up comparing the Earth's atmosphere to a giant greenhouse, with greenhouse gases as an ever-thickening blanket. Was it scientifically precise? Not entirely. But it was understandable and memorable. Her talk ended up going viral, reaching millions more people than she ever expected.

Remember, the goal of this step isn't perfection—it's impact. Do not aim for a flawless recitation; aim for a presentation that resonates, engages, and maybe even changes a few minds along the way.

And there you have it: the five steps of Rapid Prototyping. It is like CrossFit for your presentation skills, minus the risk of pulling a hamstring (unless you're really getting into that chicken suit).

Let's move forward with some practical tips and tricks to make the most of your Rapid Prototyping process.

RAPID PROTOTYPING HACKS: TURBOCHARGE YOUR PREPARATION

Alright, presentation padawans, now you've covered the five steps of Rapid Prototyping, it's time to supercharge your process with some insider tips. Think of these as the secret sauce to your presentation Big Mac. (Is that trademark infringement? Let's hope not.)

The Buddy System: Find Your Presentation Partner in Crime

Remember in elementary school when you had to hold hands with a buddy on field trips? Well, we're bringing that back, minus the hand-holding (unless that's your thing, in which case, you do you).

Find a trusted friend, colleague, or long-suffering spouse to be your presentation buddy. Their job? To be your audience, your critic, and your cheerleader all rolled into one.

Why it works:

Having an actual human to present to beats talking to your houseplants. (Though if your ficus has particularly insightful feedback, maybe keep it in the loop.)

Action:

The "Devil's Advocate" Drill. Have your buddy intentionally challenge your points, like Gladiator sparring, but with less risk of a black eye.

The Swiss Army Knife Approach: Multitask Your Practice

Who says you can only practice your presentation in front of a mirror? Not me, that's for sure. (And if someone else says that, don't listen to them. They probably still use a flip phone.)

Practice your content while doing other tasks. Recite your opening while making breakfast. Run through your main points while walking the dog. Deliver your closing argument to your shower head.

Why it works:

It helps you internalize your content in different contexts, making it more flexible and adaptable. Plus, it turns mundane tasks into productive practice time. Win-win!

Action:

The "Presentation Karaoke" challenge. Record your main points as audio clips, then play them on shuffle. Your job? Create smooth transitions between these randomly ordered points, like mental Tetris for your presentation.

The Self-Tape Experience: Film Yourself

I know, I know. Watching yourself on video is about as comfortable as a dentist appointment with the hygienist making small talk. But it's worth it.

Film your run-throughs and watch them back. Yes, you'll cringe. Yes, you'll wonder if your hair always does that weird thing. But you'll also gain invaluable insights into your presentation style.

Why it works:

It allows you to see yourself as your audience sees you. Plus, it's a great way to catch those unconscious habits. (Turns out I have a tendency to do jazz hands when I get excited. Who knew?)

Action:

The "Silent Movie" review. Watch your video on mute. Focus solely on your body language and facial expressions. You might be surprised at what you're communicating without words.

The Time Traveler's Trick: Practice in Different Durations

Your presentation is thirty minutes long? Great. Now practice giving it in fifteen minutes. Now five minutes. Now sixty seconds.

Why it works:

It forces you to identify your core message and key points. Plus, it prepares you for those, "Oops, we're running behind schedule, can you cut your talk in half?" moments.

Action:

The "Elevator Pitch" challenge. Imagine you step into an elevator and find yourself face-to-face with the CEO of your dream company. You have until the tenth floor to deliver your presentation. Go!

The Improv Comedian's Secret: Embrace the Unexpected

Fun fact: The best moments in improv comedy often come from mistakes or unexpected suggestions. The same can be true for your presentation.

Don't just practice everything going right. Practice with interruptions, tech failures, and unexpected questions.

Why it works:

It prepares you for the reality that things rarely go exactly as planned. Plus, it helps you develop the flexibility to handle curveballs with grace.

Action:

The "Plot Twist" game. Have a friend randomly interject with bizarre scenarios during your practice. "The lights just went out!" "A mariachi band just started playing outside!" Your job? Roll with it and keep your presentation going.

Remember, the goal of Rapid Prototyping isn't to create a robot-like delivery, but to make you so comfortable with your content that you can handle whatever comes your way with the cool confidence of James Bond ordering a martini. (Shaken, not stirred, in case you were wondering.)

Embrace the chaos, learn from the stumbles, and even if you forget every single one of these tips, never imagine your audience in their underwear: it's creepy, ineffective, and not the vibe.

The Final Act: Mastering the Art of Feedback and Self-Review

You're in the home stretch. You have prototyped, practiced, and probably embarrassed yourself in front of your pet a few times. But there's one final hurdle to clear: feedback.

I know what you're thinking. "Feedback? Isn't that just a fancy word for 'criticism'?" Well, not exactly. When done right, feedback is less like a punch to the gut and more like a gentle nudge in the right direction. The key is knowing how to give it, how to receive it, and most importantly, how to use it.

THE FEEDBACK TANGO: IT TAKES TWO

At some point during your Rapid Prototyping journey—whether during the Improv It, Run It, or Work It phase—you will find yourself performing in front of actual humans. If you used the *Buddy System* tip a few pages ago, you will have already got that going. Sometimes it's just to have some breathing bodies in the room (your houseplants don't count, no matter how attentive they seem). Other times, it's because you genuinely want input on what's working and what's not.

Not all feedback is created equal. As Tennessee Williams so eloquently put it, "All cruel people describe themselves as paragons of frankness." In other words, just because someone's willing to give you feedback doesn't mean they're qualified to do so.

You wouldn't invite the mailman to critique your latest interpretive dance piece (unless, of course, your mailman happens to be a former Bolshoi ballet dancer, in which case, lucky you). The same goes for your presentation. Be selective about who you involve in your creative process.

Getting the Good Stuff: A Guide to Effective Feedback

So, how do you get feedback that actually helps? Be clear, direct, and own your workshopping process. Here are some tried-and-true methods:

1. The Mark-Up Method: Give your audience a copy of your script. Ask them to circle parts where they got lost, confused, or bored. Have them underline the parts that excited them. This gives you a roadmap of your presentation's highs and lows.
2. The Five Stage Languages Rubric: Use the Five Stage Languages as a framework for feedback. Ask specific

questions about your Verbal, Vocal, Physical, Visual, and Emotional delivery.

3. The LB/NT Method: This gem comes from Maggie Bayless at ZingTrain. LB/NT stands for "liked best, next time." Have your audience write what they liked best on one side of a paper, and what they'd want more or less of next time on the reverse. It is like a pro/con list for your presentation.
4. The Throughline Takeaway: Ask your audience how they'd explain your talk to someone else, like a game of telephone, but with your presentation. You'll know quickly if the key message landed.

The Golden Rule of Feedback: Write It Down

Pro tip: Whichever feedback method you use, be sure to have your audience write it down. Give them five or ten minutes at the end of your session to gather their thoughts and put pen to paper. And if this was just an "I needed a warm body to present to" kind of session, feel free to toss those notes. Use them to line your parakeet's cage. Make a lovely origami swan. The world is your oyster.

The Power of "No": It's Okay to Decline Feedback

They don't teach you in school that it's okay to say no to feedback. If you're not ready, not interested, or already have enough to work on, you can politely decline. Take a page from my friend and client, Neen James. When someone asks, "Can I share my feedback?" she simply responds, "No. Not today." Short, sweet, and to the point.

The Journey Continues: From Workshop to Stage

Remember, the journey from workshop to stage is an ongoing process. Like directors and actors who continually explore and refine their work, you too should keep honing your craft. The goal of this entire process is to "Make a Scene"—to create moments that resonate, engage, and leave a lasting impact on your audience.

Your unique voice and perspective are what make your scenes truly unforgettable. So go forth, embrace the process, and make some magic happen.

TAKING IT BEYOND THE STAGE: YOUR 24/7 COMMUNICATION GYM

You've mastered the Rapid Prototyping process. You know how to workshop a presentation from rough concept to polished performance. But here's where many speakers stop, treating their communication skills like a suit they only take out for special occasions. Let's change that.

Why Practice Never Stops

Remember how we talked about internalizing your content rather than memorizing it? The same principle applies to your overall communication skills. The best speakers aren't just good during presentations—they're strong communicators in every situation. They've turned practice into a lifestyle.

The Everyday Communication Workout

Think of these exercises as your between-sessions training program. Just like athletes don't only exercise during games, speakers shouldn't only practice during formal preparations.

THE SUPERMARKET SOLILOQUY

- **What:** Turn each shopping aisle into a mini-presentation opportunity
- **How:** Choose a product and give a 30-second pitch about it
- **Why:** Builds your ability to structure thoughts quickly and speak about unfamiliar topics
- **Connects to:** The "Improv It (no notes)" stage of Rapid Prototyping

THE TRAFFIC LIGHT PITCH

- **What:** Use red lights as timed practice sessions
- **How:** Deliver your key messages before the light changes
- **Why:** Develops timing and concision
- **Connects to:** The "Work It" phase's emphasis on timing and delivery

THE SHOWER SINGER'S SEGUE

- **What:** Practice transitions while doing daily tasks
- **How:** Connect random topics smoothly, starting with something familiar
- **Why:** Strengthens your ability to create natural transitions
- **Connects to:** The "Improv It (with notes)" phase of finding natural connections

THE NETFLIX NARRATOR

- **What:** Mute your favorite show and provide commentary
- **How:** Describe the action as if it relates to your presentation topics
- **Why:** Enhances descriptive language and storytelling abilities
- **Connects to:** The "Read It" phase's focus on narrative flow

Making It Work

The key isn't doing all of these exercises—it's finding the ones that fit naturally into your daily routine. Choose one or two that resonate with you and make them habits. Remember:

- Start small: One exercise, consistently done, beats sporadic marathon sessions
- Stay playful: These should feel like games, not chores
- Connect the dots: Link each practice moment back to your formal Rapid Prototyping work

The Bottom Line

Your next presentation starts long before you step on stage. By weaving these micro-practices into your daily life, you're building the muscle memory that makes great communication feel effortless. When you finally do step up to present, you're not just drawing on your formal practice—you're accessing weeks or months of accumulated experience.

PiTCHES
&
PROSPECTS
PROPOSALS

CHAPTER 10

PRESENTATIONS AT WORK: PITCHES, PROPOSALS, AND PROSPECTS

(OR HOW TO MAKE YOUR BOSS SWOON WITHOUT HR GETTING INVOLVED)

> *"The best way to teach your kids about taxes is by eating 30% of their ice cream."*
>
> — **Bill Murray**

Alright, corporate crusaders and business badasses, let's take all those shiny new communication skills and put them to work where it really counts—in the cutthroat world of business presentations. I mean pitches that could make Mark Cuban weep, proposals so compelling they practically sign themselves, and sales calls that have clients throwing money at you like you're Channing Tatum in a pair of tear-away pants.

The importance of strong presentation skills in the business world can't be overstated. A Speechcraft study found that seventy percent of employed Americans who give presentations agree that presentation skills are critical to their success at work. Moreover, storytelling isn't just for entertainment—it has real business impact. According to a study by Origin/Hill Holliday, fifty-five percent of consumers are more likely to buy from brands that tell stories.

But let's get one thing straight: the business world isn't your high school debate club. It is a whole different ballgame, and the stakes are higher than Snoop Dogg at a Willie Nelson concert. Let's turn you into a lean, mean, business-presenting machine.

THE ART OF THE ELEVATOR PITCH: GOING UP?

You step into an elevator, and holy smokes, it's the CEO of your dream company. You have precisely thirty seconds to make an impression before they step off and potentially out of your life forever. What do you do? Panic and talk about the weather? Pretend to be deeply fascinated by the elevator buttons? Not on my watch, you don't.

This, my friends, is where the elevator pitch comes in—compact, versatile, and if done right, impressively effective. This is how to craft one to make even the most jaded executive sit up and take notice:

1. Hook 'em fast: Remember our lesson on the "I Want Song" from Chapter 5? This is where it pays off. Start with a grabber that makes them want to hear more.

2. Problem, solution, boom: Quickly outline a problem, present your solution, and boom—mind blown.
3. What's in it for them? Channel your inner salesperson (minus the plaid jacket, please) and highlight the benefits.
4. Call to action: End with a clear next step. A meeting, a demo, an interpretive dance showcase—whatever moves your idea forward.
5. Practice, but don't sound rehearsed: This is where our Rapid Prototyping methods come in handy. Practice your pitch in different scenarios until it feels natural.

Action:

The "Random Object" Pitch Challenge. Grab any object near you and practice pitching it as the next big thing. Can you make a stapler sound like it'll revolutionize the industry? If so, you're on the right track.

CRAFTING COMPELLING PROPOSALS: MORE THAN JUST PRETTY WORDS ON PAPER

It is time to talk about the art of putting your brilliant ideas down on paper (or more likely, in a PDF, because who uses actual paper anymore?). A great proposal is like a love letter to your potential client or boss, if that love letter included market analysis and a detailed budget breakdown.

This is how to make your proposals so irresistible, they'll sign on the dotted line before they even finish reading:

1. Know your audience: Remember your lesson on adapting your language in Chapter 5? This is where it really pays off. Tailor your proposal to your specific audience.
2. Tell a story: Use the storytelling techniques in Chapter 5 to create a narrative arc in your proposal. Take them on a journey from problem to solution.
3. Be visually appealing: Remember, we eat with our eyes first. The same goes for proposals. Use the visual language skills from Chapter 8 to make your proposal a feast for the eyes.
4. Be specific and realistic: Vague promises are as useful as a chocolate teapot. Use concrete examples and realistic projections.
5. Address objections before they arise: Anticipate potential pushback and address it head-on. It is like being a proposal psychic.

MASTERING SALES CALLS & PRESENTATIONS: TURNING "MAYBE" INTO "YES, PLEASE!"

It is April 2007 and my hands are sweating as I am about to deliver a presentation as part of an interview at Lettuce Entertain You. I look up at the four women in front of me—a VP, a Director of Training, one of the only female Master Sommeliers in the world, and the recruiter who's been advocating for them to hire me. For the last six years, I've been working at Potbelly Sandwich Shop, going from entry-level manager to directing our corporate university. Along the way, I've given thousands of trainings, workshops, and presentations—but this feels different.

For the last couple of years, I've been slowly getting more and more into wine. Reading some books. Going to tastings every week at the local wine shop. Hosting wine parties in my Chicago condo. Part of my desire to jump ship and go to Lettuce was getting to work with full-service restaurants and specifically to work with wine – so much so that I'm in front of these four women about to give a presentation on wine because I've convinced the recruiter that I am indeed a wine expert. Dear Reader: I was not.

Knowing that I am going to be presenting wine to a Master Sommelier, I realize I'm not going to get away with the normal BS I can when hosting my friends at my apartment. They are impressed I can open the bottle with a classic style corkscrew, not to say anything of my ability to tell them how a rosé is made. So, I double down on the one thing I know really well—storytelling. I focus on talking about the wine traditions and their modern applications in Mexican wines, something I realize very few people (even a Master Sommelier) are thinking about or talking about in 2007. I lean heavily on my storytelling skills and my fluency in Spanish to pronounce every varietal, valley, and viticultural term perfectly. I focus on the people, the stories, and the experiences of Valle De Guadalupe (the main region in Mexico for winemaking).

Nailed it. I got the job and was able to rapidly expand my wine knowledge to become a Sommelier myself (not a Master Sommelier but still passed several certifications in record time). I still credit my ability to tell stories and leverage the power of the Five Stage Languages. That experience led me to write and teach about wine all around the world, win a wine educator award, and be the friend you definitely want to pick out the wine the next time we have dinner.

Welcome to the thunderdome of the business world—sales calls and presentations. This is where the rubber meets the road, where the wheat is separated from the chaff, where... okay, I'll stop with the clichés. But you get the point: this is important stuff.

Here is how to turn your sales calls and presentations from snooze-fests into money-making machines:

1. Do your homework: Know your client better than they know themselves. It isn't stalking if it's for business, right? (Disclaimer: It might still be stalking. Maybe don't go through their trash). In my interview story, I knew I couldn't fool a Master Sommelier by training to our Sommelier her, so I focused on storytelling.
2. Start with a bang: Remember our lessons on grabbing attention from Chapter 5? Use them here. Start with something that makes them sit up and take notice. In my interview, I started by telling a story about a small female-owned winery in Mexico's Valle de Guadalupe.
3. Focus on benefits, not features: Your product might have more bells and whistles than a one-man band,

but what your client really cares about is how it'll make their life better.

4. Use the power of silence: Remember our discussion on the power of pauses in Chapter 6? Use strategic silences to let important points sink in and to encourage your client to talk.
5. Be prepared for anything: This is where our Rapid Prototyping methods really shine. Practice handling different scenarios and objections.

Action:

The "Worst Case Scenario" Role Play. Have a friend throw the most ridiculous objections at you during a mock sales call. If you can handle, "But what if aliens invade and steal all our computers?" you can handle anything.

ADAPTING YOUR STYLE FOR DIFFERENT BUSINESS CONTEXTS: BE LIKE WATER, MY FRIEND

Just as you wouldn't wear a tuxedo to a beach party (unless you're James Bond), you shouldn't use the same presentation style in every business context. It is all about adaptability, baby.

Here is a quick guide to adapting your style:

1. Board meetings: Channel your inner Meryl Streep in *The Devil Wears Prada*. Confident, concise, and just a touch intimidating.
2. Team presentations: Think more "Captain America rallying the Avengers" and less "Thanos threatening to destroy half the universe."
3. Client pitches: Imagine you're on *Shark Tank*, but instead of grumpy sharks, your audience is a group of friendly dolphins. Enthusiastic, but not desperate.
4. Informal business settings: Picture yourself at a backyard BBQ, but instead of discussing your neighbor's new grill, you're talking quarterly projections.

Remember, the key is to stay true to your authentic self while adjusting your energy and delivery to fit the context, like being a communication chameleon... but with better suits.

PRESENTING NUMBERS: MAKING DATA DANCE AND STATISTICS SING

It is bedtime, and I'm reading *If You Give a Mouse a Cookie* to my daughter for what feels like the 1,456th time. She is petting my face, stalling bedtime, asking for water, telling me about her school friend who likes to pretend he's a hamster who can juggle, and then, out of nowhere, she asks, "How much do you love me, Papi?" So I tell her I love her "so much." But she persists, "How ***many*** do you love me, Papi?"

Now, I'm pretty good with numbers, but how do you quantify love for your child? I can't say, "Oh, about 7.5 billion heart emojis worth," or, "Every single one of the points in my Delta SkyMiles account times infinity." And that, my friends, is the challenge we face when presenting numbers in the business world, too.

Numbers are never just numbers—they're stories waiting to be told. It is our job as communicators, whether on stages, screens, in interviews, or boardrooms, to present numbers in a way that makes sense, creates impact, and stirs emotions in our audience. Because let's face it, numbers alone are about as exciting as watching paint dry in slow motion.

Here are some rules to live by to turn your data into drama:

1. Translate Everything: Your Audience Isn't Google

When it comes to numbers, we're not just data processors—we're storytellers. Your job is to turn those cold, hard figures into a narrative that resonates. Think of yourself as the Rosetta Stone of statistics, translating complex data into a language your audience not only understands but feels.

Bad Example: "Our new process improved efficiency by thirty-seven percent."

Good Example: "Our new process saved enough time to watch the entire *Lord of the Rings* trilogy every week."

Bad Example: "The company's carbon footprint decreased by ten thousand tons last year."

Good Example: "We reduced our carbon emissions by the equivalent of taking two thousand cars off the road for a year."

2. Round With Enthusiasm: Precision Isn't Always Your Friend

In the world of numbers, sometimes less really is more. Unless you're calculating rocket trajectories for NASA, those decimal points might be doing more harm than good. Rounding your numbers can make them more digestible and memorable. Remember, aim for impact, not a math exam.

Bad Example: "Our customer satisfaction rate increased from 87.3 percent to 92.7 percent."

Good Example: "Our customer satisfaction rate increased more than 5%, to 9 out of 10 happy customers. That last guy? We're working on him."

Bad Example: "The project was completed in 67.5 days, 3.2 days ahead of schedule."

Good Example: "We finished the project a half-week early, giving us all time for an extra-long coffee break."

3. Make It Tangible: Give Them Something to Touch

Abstract numbers are like clouds—hard to grasp and quick to evaporate from memory. Your mission, should you choose to accept it, is to turn those nebulous numbers into concrete concepts. Give your audience something they can visualize, something that connects to their everyday experience.

Bad Example: "Our new server can process one petabyte of data."

Good Example: "Our new server can process enough data to store every book ever written... fifty times over."

Bad Example: "The new wind farm generates one hundred megawatts of power."

Good Example: "Our new wind farm generates enough electricity to power all the homes in Orlando, Florida."

4. Stir Those Emotions: Numbers Should Make You Feel Something

Data doesn't just inform—it can inspire, shock, or delight. When presenting numbers, don't just aim for the head; go for the heart. Use your figures to tell a story that makes your audience feel something. After all, people may forget what you said, but they'll remember how you made them feel.

Bad Example: "Deforestation affects 18.7 million acres of forest per year."

Good Example: "Every year, we lose enough forest to cover all of Ireland. Imagine a world without leprechauns or green beer!"

Bad Example: "Our product reduces workplace accidents by twenty-five percent."

Good Example: "With our product, one in four workplace injuries never happens. That's one less person who must limit their playtime with their kids, take a medical absence from work, or seek expensive medical intervention."

5. Use Familiar Landmarks: Take Them to Wrigley Field (or Fenway Park)

When dealing with large or abstract numbers, your audience needs a frame of reference. Think of it as giving them a map with familiar landmarks. By anchoring your numbers to concepts or places your audience knows well, you help them navigate the unfamiliar terrain of your data.

Bad Example: "The Great Pacific Garbage Patch is approximately 1.6 million square kilometers."

Good Example: "The Great Pacific Garbage Patch is twice the size of Texas. Imagine driving across Texas, then doing it again, but this time through a sea of plastic."

Bad Example: "The human brain processes information at sixty bits per second."

Good Example: "Your brain processes information about as fast as a 1980s modem. But unlike that modem, your brain doesn't make that awful screeching noise when it connects."

By providing these additional examples, we give readers more opportunities to see how these principles can be applied in various contexts, making the advice more versatile and actionable.

Suddenly, the vastness of cosmic time becomes comprehensible.

Your goal isn't just to inform—it's to illuminate. Give your audience more than numbers; give them a narrative. Present more than data; paint a picture. And for the love of all that is holy, please don't make them do math in their heads. That's what spreadsheets are for.

Go forth and make those numbers dance, you data-driven dynamos. Your audience (and my daughter) will thank you for it.

And there you have it, folks—your guide to slaying it in the world of business presentations. Now go forth and conquer, you magnificent corporate creatures. Just remember, with great power comes great responsibility... and hopefully a nice bonus at the end of the year.

THE LIGHTS
THE CAMERA
THE SOUND
THE LOOK
THE BACKGROUND
THE ACTION
OWN THE ZOOM

CHAPTER 11

OWN THE ZOOM: MASTERING VIRTUAL COMMUNICATION

(OR HOW TO BE MORE ENGAGING THAN A CAT VIDEO IN A WORLD OF DIGITAL DISTRACTIONS)

"I used to think that my life was going to be like a great presentation, but then I realized it's more like a Power-Point where the slides keep changing and I have no idea what's next."

— Stephen Colbert

Remember March 2020? When suddenly, the world turned upside down. Our living rooms became our offices, our cats became our coworkers (and let's be honest, probably our favorites), and our computer screens became our windows to the professional world. We entered a brave new world of virtual communication, where "You're on mute" became the catchphrase of the decade.

Fast forward to today. We swapped boardrooms for Zoom rooms, and even though the pandemic is in the rearview, we aren't going back. Hybrid work isn't just a temporary fix—it's our new reality. But fear not, my digital dynamos! Just because we've traded traditional conference rooms for virtual ones doesn't mean we can't still command attention and influence decisions. In fact, mastering the art of virtual communication might just be your secret weapon in this transformed landscape. So, let's turn you from a virtual novice into a Zoom Jedi master.

SETTING UP YOUR VIRTUAL STAGE: LIGHTS, CAMERA, WI-FI!

Remember in Chapter 8 when we talked about the importance of visual language? Well, in the virtual world, that's cranked up to eleven. Your background isn't just a backdrop anymore—it's a statement about who you are and how seriously you take this whole virtual gig.

Here is how to set up a virtual stage that screams, "I've got my act together!" (even if you're secretly wearing pajama pants):

1. Lighting is your best friend: Position yourself facing a window for natural light, or invest in a ring light. You want to glow with competence, not lurk in the shadows like a corporate gremlin.
2. Camera angle is key: Position your camera at eye level or slightly above. We want "confident professional," not "up-the-nose blogger from 2005."
3. Background check: Choose a background that's professional but not boring. A bookshelf says, "I read," while a blank wall says, "I live in a prison cell." If you must use a virtual background, for the love of all that is holy, make sure it doesn't glitch and make you look like you're phasing in and out of reality.

4. Sound matters: Invest in a good microphone. Nothing says, "I don't value your time," quite like sounding like you're talking through a drive-thru speaker from 1992.
5. Dress the part: Yes, we know you're wearing sweatpants. But from the waist up, dress as if you're meeting in person. And please, for everyone's sake, remember to wear pants. You never know when you might have to stand up.

Action:

The "First Impression" Test. Set up your virtual stage, then step away and walk back into frame as if seeing it for the first time. What is your first impression? If it's not, "Wow, this person has their act together," keep tweaking.

ENGAGING AN ONLINE AUDIENCE: FIGHTING THE SIREN SONG OF TWITTER

Ah, the online audience. They are out there somewhere, beyond the void of your screen, possibly paying attention, possibly scrolling through Instagram. Your job? To keep them so engaged they forget there's a whole internet of cat videos just a click away.

Here is how to keep your virtual audience more captivated than a toddler with an iPad:

1. Energy is everything: Remember in Chapter 6 when we talked about vocal energy? In the virtual world, crank that up to eleven. Be the human equivalent of a double espresso.
2. Use the chat function: Encourage participation through chat; it's like passing notes in class, but professional.
3. Polling for the win: Use polls to keep your audience engaged and to gather real-time feedback, like *Who Wants to Be a Millionaire*, but with less Regis Philbin and more business insights.
4. Visual aids are your friend: Use slides, props, or even costume changes (okay, maybe not that last one) to keep things visually interesting.
5. Break it up: Use breakout rooms for small group discussions, like the virtual equivalent of "turn to your neighbor and discuss," minus the awkward eye contact.

Action:

The "Multitasking Challenge." While presenting, try to spot audience members who are clearly multitasking. Then, find a way to subtly call on them or engage them directly. It is like a game of virtual whack-a-mole, but with distracted colleagues.

TECHNIQUES FOR WEBINARS AND VIRTUAL KEYNOTES: BECOMING THE NETFLIX OF BUSINESS PRESENTATIONS

Webinars and virtual keynotes are the new rock concerts of the business world, except instead of screaming fans, you have politely interested professionals. And instead of throwing roses, friendship bracelets, and teddy bears at you, they might throw a LinkedIn connection request your way. Here is how to be a virtual rock star:

1. Start with a bang: Use a provocative statement, a surprising statistic, or a compelling story to grab attention right from the start, like a virtual mic drop, but at the beginning.
2. Interaction is key: Use tools like live Q&A, real-time polls, or even virtual whiteboards to keep your audience involved, like a choose-your-own-adventure book, but for business.
3. Pacing is everything: In the virtual world, attention spans are shorter than a TikTok video. Vary your pacing, use pauses effectively, and consider breaking your content into shorter segments.
4. Be visually compelling: Your slides need to work harder in a virtual setting. Use high-quality images, animations, and even video clips to keep things visually interesting.
5. End with a clear call to action: What do you want your audience to do after the webinar? Make it clear, make it easy, and make it enticing.

Action:

The "Pause and Engage" Technique. Every ten minutes, pause your presentation and ask your audience to do something—answer a poll, type a question in the chat, or even stand up and stretch. It is a virtual palate cleanser.

OVERCOMING COMMON VIRTUAL PRESENTATION CHALLENGES: WHEN TECHNOLOGY DECIDES TO BECOME YOUR ARCH-NEMESIS

In the world of virtual presentations, Murphy's Law reigns supreme. If something can go wrong, it probably will, and probably right in the middle of your most important point. Here is how to handle common virtual villains:

1. The dreaded, "You're on mute": Have a visual cue ready (like a "You're on mute" sign) for when someone tries to talk while muted. It is like a silent movie, but for the digital age.
2. Technical difficulties: Always have a backup plan. Can you switch to phone audio? Continue via chat? Interpretive dance? (Okay, maybe not that last one.)
3. Awkward silences: In virtual meetings, silence feels ten times longer. Have some icebreaker questions or discussion prompts ready to fill any dead air.
4. The "Can everyone see my screen?" conundrum: Before sharing your screen, close unnecessary tabs or applications. Unless you want everyone to see your "Cats Wearing Hats" Pinterest board.
5. The unexpected guest appearance: Whether it's your cat walking across the keyboard or your kid bursting in to show you their latest crayon masterpiece, handle unexpected interruptions with grace and humor. It humanizes you and gives everyone a much-needed laugh.

Action:

The "Disaster Scenario" Drill. Have a friend randomly interject with common virtual presentation problems during a practice run. The more you handle these in practice, the smoother you'll be when (not if) they happen in real life.

Remember, my virtual virtuosos, the key to owning the Zoom is to embrace the medium rather than fight against it. Use its unique features to your advantage, adapt your in-person skills to the virtual world, and always, always have a backup pair of pants within reach. You never know when you might need to stand up.

Now go forth and conquer the virtual world. May your Wi-Fi be strong, your lighting be flattering, and your cat refrain from walking across your keyboard at crucial moments. You've got this!

Let's move on to Chapter 12: The Power of the Moment: Making Every Second Count (Or How to Be Unforgettable Without Accidentally Going Viral for the Wrong Reasons), which continues to build on your skills from previous chapters while focusing on these specific communication scenarios.

Q&A
PANELS
INTERVIEWS
PODCASTS

CHAPTER 12

THE POWER OF THE MOMENT: MAKING EVERY SECOND COUNT

(OR HOW TO BE UNFORGETTABLE WITHOUT ACCIDENTALLY GOING VIRAL FOR THE WRONG REASONS)

> *"What I know for sure is that speaking your truth is the most powerful tool we all have."*
>
> — **Oprah Winfrey**

Ever notice how the most memorable moments in media aren't the long speeches? They're those lightning-strike moments that have everyone grabbing their phones to tweet "Did they just say that?!" Whether you're dropping into a TV segment, joining a panel discussion, or being interviewed on a podcast, your success often hinges on making the most of tiny windows of opportunity. Think of it as speed dating for your ideas – you've got about 30 seconds to make them fall in love with your point.

THE ARCHITECTURE OF IMPACT

Here's the truth that most public speaking books won't tell you: in today's media landscape, you rarely get more than 30 seconds to make your point. The age of long-form monologues is giving way to an era of quick-strike impact. Yes, that means your teenager's ability to scroll through 50 videos in 5 minutes isn't just a sign of declining attention spans – it's actually preparation for the future of communication.

Think of these brief opportunities as diamonds: small, but incredibly valuable when cut properly. And just like diamonds, if you mess up the cutting part, you end up with very expensive dust. No pressure!

THE THREE ELEMENTS OF MEMORABLE MOMENTS

Watch any compelling media appearance and you'll notice three distinct elements working together. My client Carla reached out because she was getting ready to go on a National TV show to talk about Artificial Intelligence – a hot topic in which she has a specific angle. But she was nervous because two previous attempts at bridging the gap between what was in her head and what she ended up saying had left her without the soundbite and media clip she had hoped for. "I felt like I was throwing spaghetti at a wall," she told me afterward. "Nothing stuck." Her upcoming book, next keynote speech, and overall business model would really benefit from this big TV appearance.

That's when we broke down what I call the Moment's Trinity: the Setup, the Strike, and the Echo. Think of it like a three-act play performed in the time it takes to microwave popcorn.

THE SETUP: CREATING THE CONTAINER

The Setup isn't just an introduction – it's the frame that makes everything else make sense. Listen to Terry Gross's 2011 Fresh Air interview with Maurice Sendak, creator of "Where the Wild Things Are." She could have opened with questions about his books, his legacy, his influence on children's literature. Instead, she asked something deceptively simple: "Can you talk about what it's been like for you to grow old?"

This Setup worked because it:

- Created immediate intimacy
- Opened space for reflection rather than just recollection
- Gave Sendak permission to be present rather than just retrospective

THE STRIKE: DELIVERING THE IMPACT

The Strike is your moment of truth – where you deliver the payload that your Setup promised. But here's what most people miss: the Strike isn't about what you say; it's about what the audience feels.

Sendak's response struck deep: "I have nothing now but praise for my life. I'm not unhappy. I cry a lot because I miss people. They die and I can't stop them. They leave me and I love them more..." His voice, crackling with emotion, transformed what could have been a maudlin moment into something profound: "I am in love with the world."

The Strike worked because it:

- Delivered raw emotional truth
- Transformed personal experience into universal meaning
- Created an "I never thought about death that way" moment

THE ECHO: MAKING IT STICK

The Echo is where most people think they're done, but it's actually where the real magic happens. This is where your moment transcends the immediate and becomes part of a larger conversation.

That interview, particularly after Sendak's death the following year, became more than just a powerful radio moment. It was turned into an animated short that went viral. The phrase "I am in love with the world" became a touchstone for discussions about aging, about art, about finding joy in the face of loss. What started as a simple interview question created ripples that continue to resonate.

Creating a powerful Echo means:

- Crafting language that begs to be repeated
- Building bridges to deeper human experiences
- Leaving wisdom that others can carry forward

When these three elements work together, they create what I call a Moment Multiplier. The Setup draws people in, the Strike delivers the impact, and the Echo ensures it lives beyond the moment.

Keep in mind that your ability to master these moments is exponentially improved when you bring in the work you've done with the Five Stage Languages and Rapid Prototyping Protocol. The Five Stage Languages will help you bring the contrast and clarity needed to excel while the Rapid Prototyping Protocol will help you workshop, polish, and perfect your bits.

MASTERING DIFFERENT MEDIA FORMATS

The principles of Setup-Strike-Echo remain constant across formats, but how you apply them shifts with the medium. Let's look at how successful communicators adapt these elements to different stages.

Television's Direct Impact

Watch Anderson Cooper's September 1, 2005 CNN coverage of Hurricane Katrina - particularly his interview with Senator Mary Landrieu. In what became one of broadcast journalism's defining moments, Cooper showed how to transform righteous anger into powerful television while maintaining journalistic integrity.

The senator had just finished praising other politicians for their response efforts. Cooper, who had spent four days witnessing devastation firsthand, interrupted: "Do you get the anger that is out here?" His voice steady but intense, he continued: "For the last four days, I've been seeing dead bodies in the streets here in Mississippi... To listen to politicians thanking each other and complimenting each other, you know, I got to tell you, there are a lot of people here who are very upset."

Let's break down how this moment exemplifies our framework:

> **Setup:** "For the last four days, I've been seeing dead bodies in the streets..." Cooper establishes his credibility through direct witness. He's not arguing politics; he's reporting reality. This setup works because it's grounded in specific, verifiable experience rather than opinion.

Strike: The contrast between political praise and ground reality delivers the impact. Notice how Cooper doesn't just emote - he builds a case. Each detail he provides makes the politician's self-congratulation appear more disconnected from reality.

Echo: "Do you get the anger that is out here?" became more than just a question to one senator. It evolved into a touchstone for how journalists should challenge authority during crises. The phrase encapsulated what many viewed as a fundamental disconnect between political rhetoric and human suffering. Even today, it's referenced as a moment when broadcast journalism shifted from passive reporting to active accountability.

Television Moment Toolkit:

Ground emotion in observable facts

- Start with "I saw..." or "When I spoke to..." rather than "I feel..." or "I think..."
- Use specific numbers, locations, and timestamps when possible
- Reference concrete examples that viewers can visualize

Create contrast between official statements and ground reality

- Listen for disconnects between rhetoric and reality
- Use "Meanwhile..." transitions to highlight gaps
- Build your case with "While you say X, on the ground we see Y"
- Keep receipts: Note exact quotes you might need to reference

Maintain composure while showing appropriate feeling

- Control your voice, not your authenticity
- Let pauses do the emotional heavy lifting
- Use measured pacing to build intensity
- Practice the "slow burn" delivery: start calm, build deliberately
- Channel passion into precision, not volume

Use personal witness to challenge institutional responses

- Lead with direct experience: "What I witnessed was..."
- Build credibility through details only someone present would know
- Share human stories that illustrate system failures
- Position yourself as the viewer's eyes and ears
- Connect individual stories to broader systemic issues

Structure your responses for maximum impact

- Open with your strongest point
- Use the "3-30-3" rule: 3 seconds to hook, 30 seconds to explain, 3 points maximum
- End with a memorable line that encapsulates your message
- Have your "even if I get interrupted" point ready

The Panel Discussion Dynamic

Panel discussions present a unique challenge – you need to stand out while still being a team player. Think of it like jazz improvisation. Each player gets their solo moments, but the magic happens in how they work together.

Watch how Michelle Obama handles this on the TODAY Show's Global Girls Alliance panel in October 2018. When Savannah Guthrie asks about the global state of girls' education, Obama doesn't launch into statistics or policy. Instead, she starts with, "When I think about this, I think about my daughters..." She connects Sasha and Malia's educational opportunities to the 98 million adolescent girls worldwide who aren't in school. Then she widens the lens: "This isn't just about their loss – it's about our loss. We're losing potential doctors, CEOs, scientists..."

Framework in Action:

Setup: Personal story about her daughters creates immediate connection

Strike: The stark contrast with global statistics hits emotionally

Echo: "Their loss is our loss" becomes a rallying cry for action

Panel Power Moves: Start personal, then go universal

- Open with "In my experience..." or "What I've seen..."
- Connect your personal story to the larger issue within 30 seconds
- Use "bridge phrases" like "And this isn't just my story..." or "This speaks to a broader trend..."

- Choose personal stories that illuminate universal truths
- Keep your opening anecdote under 20 seconds

Use statistics as punctuation, not the main story

- Lead with the human element, follow with the numbers
- Package statistics in memorable ways: "That's like filling Madison Square Garden three times"
- Use numbers as "punctuation marks" to underscore emotional points
- Limit yourself to one or two key statistics per response
- Practice translating complex data into conversational language

Create phrases worthy of headlines

- Craft sound bites that work both in and out of context
- Use metaphors that make complex ideas tangible
- Think in tweet-sized segments (memorable 280-character thoughts)
- Create "callback phrases" you can repeat for emphasis
- Master the "period at the end of the sentence" delivery

Build bridges between other panelists' points

- Listen actively and take quick notes
- Use phrases like "Building on what Sarah said..." or "To connect this to John's point..."
- Find the complementary angle to others' perspectives
- Save key examples that can link multiple viewpoints
- Position yourself as a synthesizer of ideas

Command attention through contrast

- Vary your speaking pace and energy level
- Use strategic pauses after key points
- Shift between analytical and emotional appeals
- Change up your delivery style: lean in for intensity, sit back for reflection
- Master the "pattern interrupt" - know when to break format

Own your expertise while staying collaborative

- Acknowledge others' expertise before adding yours
- Use "Yes, and..." instead of "Yes, but..."
- Share credit generously
- Position disagreements as different perspectives rather than corrections
- Keep a mental timer - aim for 20% contribution in a five-person panel

Podcast Intimacy

Podcasts change everything about how you need to think about your moments. The intimacy of the medium – literally speaking into someone's ears – demands a different kind of presence.

Consider Marc Maron's 2010 WTF interview with Robin Williams (Episode 67). Instead of starting with Williams' filmography or his latest projects, Maron opened by acknowledging their shared history with addiction and recovery. This choice transformed what could have been just another celebrity interview into an intimate conversation about life, struggles, and redemption.

Framework in Podcasting:

Setup: Creating safety through shared vulnerability (The Maron Method)

Strike: Allowing silence and emotion to carry meaning

Echo: The conversation became one of WTF's most referenced episodes, showing how authentic connection creates lasting impact

Let's look at how others master this format:

Setup in Podcasting:

Look at how Terry Gross opens her 2019 Fresh Air interview with Tom Hanks. Instead of diving into "A Beautiful Day in the Neighborhood," she begins with: "When you started playing Fred Rogers, did you learn things about yourself?" This setup creates immediate depth, moving past promotion into personal territory.

Strike in Podcasting:

Consider how David Letterman handles striking moments on his "My Next Guest Needs No Introduction." In his 2018 interview with Barack Obama, he doesn't interrupt when silence falls after a powerful answer. Instead, he lets the moment breathe – something unique to the podcast medium where time flows differently than broadcast TV.

Echo in Podcasting:

Desert Island Discs' Kirsty Young masters the art of creating echo moments through musical choices. When interviewing Tom Hanks (2016), she played a piece that reminded him of his late mother, leading to an unplanned but profound discussion about loss.

PODCAST PRESENCE PRINCIPLES:

Create safety before depth

- Share a relevant personal story in your first few minutes
- Acknowledge common ground early: "Like you, I've experienced..."
- Use "preview statements" to telegraph deeper topics: "I'd love to explore with you..."
- Match your conversation partner's energy level
- Start with lighter topics before diving deep
- Build trust through active listening cues ("mm-hmm," "yes," soft agreements)

Let silence do the heavy lifting

- Resist the urge to fill every pause
- Count to three internally after powerful statements
- Use "intentional silence" to emphasize important points
- Watch for verbal and non-verbal cues that signal deeper thought
- Practice comfortable silence in your prep
- Remember: Podcast silence feels half as long to listeners as it does to you

Use the medium's intimacy to your advantage

- Speak as if talking to one person, not an audience
- Lower your voice slightly for more intimate moments
- Share specific details that create mental pictures
- Use sensory language: "I can still smell..." "I remember the sound of..."

- Maintain conversational tone even when making complex points
- Create "driveway moments" - stories so compelling listeners stay in their cars

Build bridges to universal experiences

- Connect personal stories to shared human experiences
- Use phrases like "You know that feeling when..."
- Transform specific incidents into universal lessons
- Look for the emotional truth in every story
- Create metaphors that make complex ideas relatable
- Draw parallels between your experience and the listener's life

Master the micro-moment

- Use verbal timestamps: "In that moment..." "Right then..."
- Slow down for important details
- Paint pictures with words: "I was standing there, coffee in hand..."
- Break big stories into digestible scenes
- Create "callback moments" to earlier parts of the conversation
- End important points with a beat of reflection

Navigate emotional territory

- Telegraph emotional content: "This next part is difficult to talk about..."

- Use authentic vulnerability rather than performative emotion
- Balance heavy moments with lighter ones
- Maintain composure while showing feeling
- Create safe "exit ramps" from intense topics
- Remember you're having a conversation, not giving a performance

Q&A Mastery: Turning Questions into Opportunities

If media appearances are like jazz improvisation, Q&A sessions are like freestyle rap battles – you never know exactly what's coming, but you need to be ready to respond with rhythm and purpose. This is where preparation and presence collide.

Let's examine three common Q&A scenarios that every public speaker faces, and how to transform each into a powerful moment:

The Hostile Question

We've all been there: You've just finished your keynote on innovation, and someone stands up with that unmistakable "actually..." energy. "Don't all these disruptions you're celebrating actually destroy more jobs than they create?"

Framework in Action:

> **Setup:** "Thank you for raising what's probably the most crucial ethical question in innovation today."
>
> **Strike:** "Let me share what I discovered when I interviewed 100 workers whose jobs were automated..."
>
> **Echo:** "Innovation without a conscience isn't progress - it's just change."

Notice how this approach:

- Validates the concern without accepting the premise
- Uses real research to ground the response
- Creates a quotable moment that advances your message

The Off-Topic Question

You're promoting your book about leadership, and someone asks about a trending news story that's barely related to your topic.

Framework in Action:

> **Setup:** "That's a fascinating parallel to what we're discussing..."
>
> **Strike:** "In my research on leadership transitions, I found a similar pattern..."
>
> **Echo:** "It all comes back to how we handle moments of uncertainty."

This strategy:

- Bridges gracefully back to your expertise
- Adds value even when redirecting
- Maintains your position as a thought leader

The Oversimplified Question

Your work is nuanced, but the question reduces it to a simple either/or: "So are you saying leaders should always be transparent?"

Framework in Action:

> **Setup:** "The real power of transparency comes not from the 'whether' but from the 'how'..."
>
> **Strike:** "Let me share a story that changed my entire perspective on this..."
>
> **Echo:** "Effective transparency isn't about sharing everything; it's about sharing what matters at the moment it matters most."

This approach:

- Elevates the conversation
- Demonstrates deeper expertise
- Creates a memorable principle

Q&A Success Strategies:

- Turn challenges into opportunities to demonstrate depth
- Use stories to bridge from their question to your message
- Create quotable moments even in spontaneous responses
- Always bring it back to value for the audience

Key Insight: The goal in Q&A isn't to answer questions; it's to address concerns. Questions are often proxies for deeper issues. When you respond to the concern behind the question, you create moments that matter.

The Setup-Strike-Echo framework is particularly powerful in Q&A because it helps you:

- Acknowledge the questioner (Setup)
- Deliver value to the entire audience (Strike)
- Leave them with something memorable (Echo)

Remember: In Q&A, you're not defending; you're revealing. You're not fighting; you're inviting others into your thinking process. Every question is an opportunity to demonstrate not just what you know, but how you think.

BREAKING DOWN CULTURAL MOMENTS: WHEN SETUP-STRIKE-ECHO MAKES HISTORY

Some moments transcend their original context to become cultural touchstones. Let's examine three distinctly different but equally powerful moments that demonstrate how our framework operates at the highest levels.

THE INSTANT ICON: MICHELLE YEOH'S OSCAR TRIUMPH

When Michelle Yeoh took the Oscar stage in March 2023, accepting her historic Academy Award as the first Asian woman to win Best Actress in the ceremony's ninety-five-year history, she transformed what could have been just another acceptance speech into a masterclass in cultural impact.

Framework Breakdown:

Setup: Watch her precise architecture. First, personal acknowledgment: "Thank you. Thank you. This is proof that dreams – dream big and dreams do come true." Then, she immediately widens the lens: "For all the little boys and girls who look like me watching tonight, this is a beacon of hope and possibilities."

Strike: At sixty, winning for *Everything Everywhere All At Once*, she delivered what became the speech's defining moment: "Ladies, don't let anybody tell you you are ever past your prime." The line landed with particular force because she had earned the right to say it, standing there with her first Oscar nomination and win.

Echo: She closed by bringing it home, literally, with a dedication to her mother watching in Malaysia: "I'm taking this home to her. She's eighty-four, and I'm taking this home to her." This personal touch completed the journey from individual achievement to universal meaning and back to family.

THE LEGACY BUILDER: AUDRA MCDONALD'S TONY MOMENT

When Audra McDonald stepped onto the Tony Awards stage in 2014, she was already making history as the first performer to win in all four acting categories. But through masterful framing, she transformed a statistical achievement into a moment of cultural resonance.

Framework Breakdown:

Setup: Rather than leading with the historic nature of her win, she begins with family: "I want to thank my mom and my dad up in heaven for disobeying the doctor's orders and not medicating their hyperactive girl and finding out what she was into instead." This immediately humanizes what could have been just another awards show moment.

Strike: Playing Billie Holiday in *Lady Day at Emerson's Bar & Grill* wasn't just another role - it was a bridge to history: "I am standing on Lena Horne's shoulders. I am standing on Maya Angelou's shoulders. I am standing on Diahann Carroll and Ruby Dee, and most of all, Billie Holiday. You deserved so much more than you were given when you were on this planet."

Echo: By connecting her record-breaking sixth Tony win to the pioneers who made it possible, McDonald transformed an individual achievement into a moment of collective recognition.

THE TIME CAPSULE: RITA MORENO'S ELEVEN WORDS

Sometimes the most powerful cultural moments come in the smallest packages. When Rita Moreno won her Oscar for *West Side Story* in 1962, becoming the first Latina to win an Academy Award, her entire speech was just eleven words: "I can't believe it! Good Lord! I leave you with that."

Framework Breakdown:

Setup: The power wasn't in carefully crafted rhetoric. Looking stunning in her black and gold gown, Moreno's visible shock said more than a prepared speech could. Her "I can't believe it!" wasn't just an expression of joy

– it was the voice of someone who never saw this path as possible.

Strike: The brevity itself was the strike. In a ceremony known for long-winded speeches, her pure, unfiltered emotion cut through. As she would later reflect in her 2021 documentary: "I couldn't believe it. I kept saying 'I don't believe it.' And that was my entire speech. I was the very first Hispanic to win an Oscar."

Echo: What makes this moment fascinating is how its echo has grown over decades. Each milestone in her journey to EGOT status – the Grammy in 1972, Tony in 1975, Emmy in 1977 – added new resonance to those eleven words. Her brief moment of disbelief became a symbol of doors opening, of possibilities expanding.

Cultural Analysis Success Strategies:

- Watch how speakers move between personal and universal meaning
- Notice how authentic emotion anchors scripted moments
- Observe how historical context amplifies impact
- Study how speakers connect individual achievement to larger significance
- Track how moments gain meaning through time
- Recognize when brevity can outweigh preparation

The key insight across all these moments is how they transcend their immediate circumstance. They're not just speeches; they're cultural inflection points where personal achievement meets collective meaning.

BRINGING IT ALL TOGETHER: FROM FRAMEWORK TO PRACTICE

The beauty of the Setup-Strike-Echo framework lies in its adaptability. Whether you're on CNN, a conference panel, or accepting an award, your goal remains the same: create moments that matter.

Remember Carla from our opening? She went back on national TV a few weeks after our work together. This time, instead of throwing spaghetti at a wall, she orchestrated a symphony. She took a complex topic – artificial intelligence ethics – and distilled it into a moment everyone was talking about the next day. "AI isn't just changing how we work," she said, pausing just long enough to let the setup land. "It's changing how we need to think about being human."

The Setup drew people in. The Strike made them think. The Echo? Her words were quoted in three major industry publications the next week. This is what's possible when you make every second count.

YOUR MOMENT-MAKING TOOLKIT

FOR TELEVISION:

- Ground every emotional moment in observable fact
- Create clear contrasts that illustrate your point
- Use personal witness to establish credibility
- Keep your key message to thirty seconds or less

FOR PANELS:

- Start personal, then go universal
- Build bridges between other panelists' points
- Create headline-worthy phrases
- Stay actively engaged even when not speaking

FOR PODCASTS:

- Create safety before seeking depth
- Let silence do heavy lifting
- Use the medium's intimacy to your advantage
- Build bridges to universal experiences

FOR Q&A:

- Turn challenges into opportunities
- Address the concern behind the question
- Create quotable moments even in spontaneous responses
- Always bring it back to audience value

FOR CULTURAL MOMENTS:

- Connect personal achievement to larger meaning
- Let authentic emotion anchor scripted remarks
- Use historical context to amplify impact
- Recognize when brevity outweighs preparation

THE BIGGER PICTURE

These aren't just techniques for looking good on camera or sounding smart on panels. They're tools for making your truth undeniable, your impact unforgettable, and your legacy indelible. The goal isn't to handle the interview; it's to forget it's an interview.

Your voice, your truth, your moments—they matter. Not just for you, but for everyone who needs to hear exactly what you have to say, exactly the way only you can say it.

AND FINALLY... (THE TRUTH BEHIND THE MAGIC)

All this preparation, all these techniques, they're not about creating a fake version of yourself. They're about being so prepared that your authentic self can shine through even under the brightest lights or the highest pressure. It's like hosting that perfect dinner party—all the prep happens in the kitchen, but when guests arrive, you're just being yourself. A very well-prepared, totally-not-frantically-Googling-how-to-put-out-kitchen-fires version of yourself.

Action:

> Start your Moment Journal today. When you see someone nail it—really nail it—write down what worked. What made you lean in? What made you remember? What made you change? That's your personal masterclass in making moments matter.

Now go make your moments count. And yes, if you go viral, make sure it's the kind of viral that makes your mother proud, your mentors nod, and your future self thank you.

the SPOTLIGHT is READY
STEP UP
SPEAK OUT
MAKE YOUR
SCENE

CONCLUSION

THE DEFIANT VOICE: IDINA MENZEL'S SYMPHONY OF RESILIENCE

(OR HOW TO LET IT GO WHEN LIFE CALLS YOU ADELE DAZEEM)

> *"It's not how you hit the high notes, it's how you recover from the missed ones."*
>
> — **Idina Menzel**

On a glamorous evening at the 2014 Academy Awards, Idina Menzel stood backstage, preparing for the biggest performance of her career. Then came the now-infamous moment when John Travolta introduced her as "Adele Dazeem." The world held its breath, wondering how she'd react. But Idina didn't miss a beat. She owned that stage, delivering a performance of "Let It Go" that left the audience in awe.

The year would hold more challenges. When New Year's Eve arrived, millions of viewers tuned in to watch Idina perform "Let It Go" on New Year's Rockin' Eve. As she approached the song's iconic high note, something unexpected happened—she didn't quite hit it. In an instant, Twitter exploded with criticism, and the press had a field day. For many performers, this could have been a crushing blow. But Idina? She took it in stride, proving once again that she was a true professional who could rise above any setback.

But the story doesn't end there. In 2023, during a concert in Orlando, Idina faced the high note in "Let It Go" once again. This time, when she didn't hit it perfectly, she stopped the song. "I can't mess this up," she joked. "It's like the Star-Spangled Banner!" Then, in a moment of pure Idina magic, she turned to the audience and said, "Why don't you all try to sing it?" The crowd responded with gusto, nailing the note. Idina's response? She flipped them off—playfully, of course—in a moment of shared laughter and camaraderie.

Later, in her 2024 tour, Idina took all these moments—the mispronunciation, the missed notes, the criticism—and wove them into her performance. She showed clips of the Oscars mishap, mimicked Travolta's introduction, and even embraced the nickname "Adele Dazeem." But then, she transitioned into a soul-stirring rendition of "Let It Go," reminding everyone that no matter how the world tries to mislabel or criticize you, you have the power to own your story and rise above it.

Idina Menzel's journey is more than a series of performances; it's a testament to the power of resilience, authenticity, and the courage to make a scene—even when (especially when) things don't go as planned. She took the moments that could have defeated her and turned them into her greatest strengths.

YOUR SYMPHONY AWAITS

> *"Let your own light shine, find your voice, and let it sing out into the world."*
>
> **— Idina Menzel**

As you reach the final pages of this book, think back to Idina Menzel's story. Remember how she took every challenge, every mishap, every criticism, and wove them into a powerful narrative of resilience and authenticity. That is the power you now hold in your hands.

When you first opened this book, you were promised a framework for sharing your messages, ideas, and stories in a way that keeps people interested, intrigued, and impacted. Now, as you close these pages, you're not just equipped with techniques and strategies—you're armed with the power to turn your life's moments, both triumphant and challenging, into compelling scenes that resonate with others.

You have learned to master the Five Stage Languages, to rapid prototype your presentations, and to find the extraordinary in the ordinary. More than that, you've discovered the courage to be authentically you—to let your voice ring out, even when it might crack on the high notes.

This journey hasn't just been about becoming a better communicator. It has been about becoming a more authentic version of yourself. It has been about creating space for truth, for genuine expression, for showing up as your full, magnificent self, just as Idina did time and time again.

Your newfound skills aren't party tricks to impress an audience, but tools to change the world, one story at a time. Your voice has the power to inspire, to challenge, to comfort, to ignite change. Your stories can be the bridge that connects hearts and minds, that helps others see the world through new eyes.

So, what will your next scene be? How will you use your voice to make a difference? What moments in your life—the triumphs, the failures, the embarrassments, the joys—will you weave into your narrative to touch others?

The world doesn't need another perfect, polished presenter. It needs you, with all your quirks, your unique experiences, your personal flavor of brilliance. Your authenticity is your superpower. Your vulnerability is your strength. Your story, in all its messy, beautiful complexity, is your gift to the world.

Remember that video you recorded at the beginning of this journey? The one where you introduced yourself and shared your mission? Now is the time to revisit it. Go ahead, I'll wait.

... *(imagine Mike sitting casually in his Director chair as his star performer readies for the grande finale)...*

Welcome back. What did you notice? Perhaps you shook your head a little at your initial awkwardness, or maybe you were surprised by how much potential you already had. But more importantly, can you see how far you've come?

That person in the video was just beginning this journey. Now, armed with the tools and confidence you've gained, imagine how you'd approach that same task today. Your posture would be more assured, your words more impactful, your presence more magnetic. You have grown from someone hesitant to share their story into a scene-maker ready to captivate an audience.

So here's a challenge: Record that video again. Introduce yourself, share your mission, tell us why you do what you do. Then compare it to your first attempt. The difference you'll see isn't just about technique – it comes from the confidence of owning your story and knowing how to share it effectively. You will also notice how you can identify—using the Five Stage Languages—the specific levers and choices you make in the video.

This before-and-after comparison isn't just an exercise—it's proof of your transformation and that the Rapid Prototyping Protocol helps you unlock the most dynamic version of yourself and gives you a repeatable process to continue to evolve, refine, and uplevel your skills. It is evidence that you're ready to step onto whatever stage awaits you, be it a boardroom, a conference hall, or a social media platform.

The stage is set. The spotlight is ready. Your audience is waiting. Step up, speak out, and make your scene. Don't wait for the perfect moment—create it. Don't shy away from the high notes—embrace them, and if you miss, let your audience sing with you.

You have within you stories that can inspire, ideas that can transform, and a voice that deserves to be heard. Don't let them remain untold. Don't let your potential for impact go unrealized.

Go forth and make some noise. Be bold. Be authentic. Be you. Let it go, let it show, let the world know the real you.

Your symphony awaits. Now, go make a scene!

> *"That's all."*
>
> **– Miranda Priestly, Devil Wears Prada**

TAKE A BOW (FORMERLY KNOWN AS "THE ACKNOWLEDGMENTS")

(OR THE PART WHERE I THANK ALL THE PEOPLE WHO KEPT ME FROM JOINING AN ASHRAM AS I WROTE THIS BOOK)

This is going to feel dramatic—but if you've made it this far with me, you know that's not exactly out of character. Taylor Swift once sang about "this godforsaken mess that you made me," and writing this book felt exactly like that—except I made the mess all by myself. The last two years have been a masterclass in creative destruction. I wrote two completely different versions of this book, a screenplay, and a novel. But this one? This one required me to break down completely before I could rebuild. They say making art requires giving pieces of yourself away, but they don't tell you how many people you need in your corner to help you stay whole.

In this production of "How to Write a Book While Simultaneously Having an Existential Crisis," the cast has been nothing short of extraordinary:

In the role of "The Anchor," Phil Fox: You don't get the shiny version of me that excites audiences on stage, or the nurturing version that holds space for clients, or even the version that remembers to listen more than talk. You get the raw footage, the dress rehearsals, the three am rewrites, and lately, the chaotic whirlwind of a husband whose business decided to explode right as he was finishing a book. You've stood with me against storms of all kinds—sea water, sand, wintry ice—and kept walking, just like you did on that first snowy Chicago night twenty years ago when we were just two boys braving a blizzard, not knowing we were starting our own epic story. Through my endless pivots, rewrites, and reinventions, you've been both catalyst and shelter, pushing me to grow while providing safe harbor for my storms. Even when I've been a hurricane of missed dinners, late-night typing sessions, and emotional plot twists during this wild 2024 glow-up, you've remained steadfast—a north star in the chaos. The depth of my gratitude to you is infinite, not just for being my partner in this beautiful mess, but for being the extraordinary father you are to Vivi. You make both of us better, and somehow, you've managed to love both the person you met in that blizzard and all the versions I've become since. Here's to twenty years of first dates, and to all the scenes yet to come.

Speaking of scene-stealers, Viviana Fox: My little Leo superstar, already outshining me at four. This book's for you, chica. I promise to keep up and be the best Stage Papi that's ever Stage Papi'd to whatever scenes you decide to make. No one has positively altered my life like you have since you first arrived on set. I love you.

And every good scene requires two brilliant stars. Ziggy Jane: You shine in every room you walk into, and I'm so thankful you are Viviana's first best friend. I'm enjoying my front row seat to your childhood and I can't wait to see what you create next. Your laugh is one of my favorites, and in your eyes, entire galaxies seem to be born every day. I love you.

In the role of "The Truth-Teller Supreme," Elizabeth Cortez: You've been stage managing the behind-the-scenes drama of my life with a Tony-worthy combination of brutal honesty and boundless love. When I needed a reality check, you delivered your lines with perfect timing (yes, the "Ice Queen" monologue was particularly memorable). You've played every supporting role imaginable—counselor, confidante, cheerleader, and chief chaos coordinator—while our daughters wrote their own friendship subplot that brought us even closer. Your ability to simultaneously call me on my nonsense and build me back up has made you the most valuable player in this production. You're the one person who can tell me I'm being absolutely awful and have me thanking you for it five minutes later. ILYSM!

In the role of "The Boss," Laura Gassner Otting: You've run this show like a perfectly orchestrated production—always producing from the wings when needed, always commanding the right scene. "Showing up! It's what she does." But it's more than that—you've mentored me while holding me accountable, then cut through the red tape of my self-doubt until I saw my own center stage potential. You've shown me both my authority and my blind spots, pushing me to level up while providing backup when I stumble. Having you in my corner feels like having a secret weapon in the theater of life, and I'm eternally grateful for your powerful, unwavering friendship. You made this book significantly more impactful than I could've made it without you. Thank you. I love you.

Playing "The Daylight," Marisa Corcoran: My heart is brighter for having you in it. You've been a lifeline these past two years, creating a space where my unhealed places could breathe and grow. I'd make a Taylor Swift pun here, but I know All Too Well that you're probably Shaking It Off right now. You've helped me step out of the woods and into the daylight, and I'm forever grateful for the way you've been there through my darkest nights to help me find my way back to the sun. The Afterglow is a total vibe.

In the role of "The Book Whisperer," Deanne Adams: You're either a therapist moonlighting as a developmental editor or you've somehow mastered both crafts simultaneously. Your tenderness and wisdom helped shape not just this book, but the writer I became in the process. Thank you for hearing what I was trying to say even when I couldn't find the words.

Playing "The Confidence Fairy Godfather," Sam Ruhmkorff: You fished me out of the "send to archive" bin and convinced me to double down on my voice. Your belief in this book when I'd lost my own helped bring it back to life. Sometimes the best editing isn't about changing words—it's about changing minds.

In the role of "Visual Storyteller," Ryan Stiner: Your illustrations bring a playful sophistication to these pages that I've admired since first seeing your work at Zingerman's. Thank you for saying yes to this project on a very brutal deadline and helping bring these ideas to life in ways words alone never could.

Playing "The Energy Maven," Erin King: From haunted Airbnbs to yacht club shenanigans, you've listened to me "wine" about everything and just keep filling my glass. Our friendship has aged like a fine wine, and I'm grape-ful for every moment. Your spirit is vintage but your energy never ages—here's to many more years of popping ideas (and corks) together, my favorite wine-ing partner!

Playing "The Sparkle Strategist," Neen James: You've been my effervescent Aussie friend, turning business dreams into standing ovations with your signature fizz. Like any great Producer, you've known when to push and when to pop the champagne. Being your Keynote Director is premier, but being your friend is Grand Cru. Cheers, mate.

To my family: Mom (Mindy Smith) and Dan Head, Granny (the OG scene-maker), Jennifer Ganino (my first scene partner), Levi, Serenity, and Stephanie Ganino; Chloe DiVita; Alice Gromada, Brandon "Cousin Burger" Gromada, and Mia Fox; Devin Cortez, Mary Gorman Sullens, and Katie Sullens; Laurette and Skip Farmer.

To the professional village: Carol Wright (publishing fairy godmother extraordinaire), Dani Wallace (who pushed me to finish), Elizabeth Goddard (who reimagined my business with me), Jessica Abo (my long-lost twin), Dusti Arab (my theater sister), Jessica Manuszak (my favorite pickle), Hillary Weiss Presswood (my Taurean queen), Katie Lance (one of my first speaker friends), Matthew Kimberly (for being a stud).

And to my dear clients: The Speakers' Guild Members (Tiffany Lanier, Melanie Weller, Jacquette M Timmons, Kim Tottori, Mandy Irby, Dana V Adams), Mike Drop Method Clients, and The Mike Drop Era Retreat 2025 ticketholders: Abhi Golhar, Barbara Schreihans, Erin Lindstrom, Jocelyn Manzanarez, Kristen Day, Chelsea Husum, Susan Drumm, Carla Johnson, Lindsey Kaszuba, Lisa Robbin Young, Laura Yaeger, and Adrienne Jamail.

Take a bow—you've earned it.

ABOUT THE AUTHOR (OR CONFESSIONS OF A PROFESSIONAL ATTENTION WHORE)

Mike Ganino is a man of many talents—think Renaissance man, but with better wine recommendations. From slinging sandwiches as a restaurant manager to slinging Shakespearean verse in improvised performances, Mike's career has more twists than a corkscrew (which he wields with sommelier-level expertise given his experience as an actual Sommelier and wine educator).

After selling his restaurant company to private equity (because who doesn't dream of turning burritos into stock options?), Mike pivoted to the world of public speaking faster than you can say, "Exit, pursued by a bear." If you have read this far and get that reference–go to **www.mikeganino.com/pursuedbybear** for a special gift. He has shared stages with celebrity chefs, reality TV stars, and even an alligator (the alligator, unsurprisingly, had little to say).

As a keynote speaker and consultant, Mike has helped companies like Netflix, Disney, and Adobe tell better stories—without resorting to, "Once upon a time," or, "In a galaxy far, far away." Let's be honest, they have already nailed those ones. He's trained over five thousand speakers, written *Company Culture for Dummies* (no dummies were harmed in the process), and was even a contestant on *American Idol* and *Popstars* (sadly, his pop career was short-lived, but his hair game remains strong).

When not teaching people to "make a scene" (in the best possible way), Mike can be found sipping wine, spoiling his daughter Viviana with Crocs, and trying to convince his dog Elliott to appreciate the finer points of improvised Tennessee Williams. No matter how "Brando" Mike screams "Stellaaaaa" —Elliott remains unimpressed.

Mike splits his time between Los Angeles, New York City, and Barcelona—or at least he would if he could figure out how to be in three places at once. For now, he settles for being omnipresent in the world of storytelling and communication (and probably on your favorite podcast).

Remember, as Mike always says, "Think smaller"—unless you're thinking about the impact you can make with your voice. In that case, think bigger. Much bigger. And don't forget the inner juice!

pssst... I have a Shakespeare-themed tattoo on my right arm. The skeleton (Hamlet), dagger (Macbeth), and poison (Romeo & Juliet) are all featured in the tattoo, so it's a little Easter egg of sorts in the book for all of you who have read this part.

ABOUT THE MIKE DROP METHOD

(OR THE ART OF MAKING PEOPLE FORGET YOU USED TO SAY "UM" EVERY OTHER WORD)

So, you've made it this far and you're thinking, "This Mike guy seems to know his stuff. How can I get some of that magic?" Well, you're in luck! The Mike Drop Method isn't just a catchy name (though it is pretty catchy, right?). It is a full-blown system for turning ordinary mortals into captivating speakers, minus the radioactive spider bite.

Here is how you can get your hands on some of that Mike Drop magic.

IN-PERSON RETREATS AND IMMERSIONS: THE MIKE DROP METHOD IMMERSIVE

(aka "Story, Speak, and Sip" weekends)

You, a group of like-minded speakers, and yours truly, locked in a room (okay, a bougie hotel or my swanky midcentury LA Director's Office) for a few days of intensive speaking training. We'll laugh, we'll cry, we'll probably drink some wine (remember, I'm a sommelier), and by the end, you'll be ready to command any stage. Warning: Side effects may include spontaneous storytelling and an irresistible urge to "make a scene" in elevators.

PRIVATE COACHING VIP DAYS: THE KEYNOTE DIRECTING EXPERIENCE

(Because who doesn't want to be a VIP?)

For those who prefer their Mike Drop Method straight up, no chaser, there's the VIP Day experience. It's just you, me, and a couple of days dedicated to transforming your speaking skills. We will dive deep into your content, polish your delivery, and maybe even work on your power pose. By the end of the day, you'll be ready to take on the world—or at least that big presentation next week.

COURSES + ONLINE WORKSHOPS

(For when you want to learn in your pajamas)

Not ready to commit to in-person training? No problem! The Mike Drop Method comes in digital flavors too. From on-demand courses that let you learn at your own pace (perfect for those three am inspiration strikes) to live online workshops where you can interact with me in real time (yes, I'm just as charming on Zoom—didn't you read that chapter already?), there's an option for everyone.

CORPORATE TRAINING + KEYNOTES

(Because even Disney needs a little extra magic sometimes)

Think your company could use a dose of the Mike Drop Method? You're in good company. I have sprinkled my communication fairy dust on some of the biggest names in the business world. From helping Disney executives tell stories that would make even Moana's Grandma jealous, to teaching Adobe teams to design presentations as sleek as their software, I've done it all.

Need a keynote that will wake up even the most jet-lagged conference attendees? I've got you covered. Just ask the folks at Netflix—I helped them binge on better communication skills faster than you can say, "Are you still watching?" And let's not forget the American Cancer Association, where I proved that even serious topics can benefit from a little humor and a lot of heart.

Whether it's rallying the troops at Caesars Entertainment (no, not with free chips), or helping Virginia Trial Lawyers Association object to boring presentations, I bring the Mike Drop Method to companies big and small. The result? Teams that communicate with the precision of a Swiss watch and the excitement of a Vegas show.

So, whether you need a keynote that will have your audience at the edge of their seats, or a workshop to transform your team into communication ninjas, I'm your guy. Just remember, what happens in a Mike Ganino corporate training, stays... incredibly useful for years to come.

Whether you're aiming to deliver a keynote that brings the house down, pitch an idea that makes investors throw money at you like you're Demi Moore, or simply stop saying "um" every other word, the Mike Drop Method has got you covered.

What are you waiting for? It's time to drop the mic—figuratively, of course. Those things are expensive.

Visit **www.mikeganino.com** to learn more about how you can work with Mike and start your journey to becoming a speaking superstar. ***Warning: May cause sudden outbursts of confidence and an inexplicable desire to volunteer for presentations.***

DELETED SCENES: THE DIRECTOR'S CUT - YOUR BLOCKBUSTER STORY CHECKLIST

(OR HOW TO MAKE SURE YOUR LIFE STORY ISN'T JUST A BUNCH OF B-ROLL)

My future Spielbergs of storytelling, put your director's hat *back* on and make sure your story is ready for its red carpet debut. This isn't just any checklist—it's your secret weapon for crafting tales that'll make your audience forget they're not actually watching a Hollywood blockbuster. (Popcorn not included, but highly recommended.)

CHARACTER(S): THE STARS OF YOUR SHOW

- Essence: Your story needs a main character who changes more than their socks. Their journey is the heart of your tale.
- Clarity: Keep your cast lean and mean. If a character doesn't serve the story, they're just taking up valuable mental real estate.

Ask yourself: Is my main character more interesting than a pet rock? If not, it's time for a rewrite.

PURPOSE OF CHARACTERS: NO EXTRAS ALLOWED

- Focus: Every character should earn their keep. If they're not moving the story forward, they're moving it backward.

Ask yourself: If this character was abducted by aliens mid-story, would anyone notice? If not, it's time for some script edits.

THE OBJECTIVE: THE "I WANT" SONG

- Goal: Pinpoint the moment your character realizes they want something different. It is like their personal "Part of Your World" moment, minus the fins.

Ask yourself: What does your character want so badly, they'd trade their voice to a sea witch to get it? (Metaphorically speaking, of course.)

START AS LATE AS POSSIBLE (EN MEDIA RES): SKIP THE BORING BITS

- Efficiency: Start your story where the action is. Nobody needs to know what your character had for breakfast... unless it was laced with truth serum.

Ask yourself: If this were a movie, would the audience still be awake by this point? If not, cut to the chase!

QUESTIONS VS. ANSWERS: KEEP 'EM GUESSING

- Intrigue: Start with questions, not a PowerPoint presentation of facts. Mystery is the secret sauce of storytelling.

Ask yourself: Am I being more mysterious than the ingredients in a hot dog, or as transparent as glass?

AVOIDING OVER-REVELATION: THE GOLDILOCKS ZONE

- Balance: Don't reveal too much (boring) or too little (confusing). Aim for juuust right.

Ask yourself: If my story were a striptease, am I revealing too much too soon, or leaving the audience out in the cold?

CONTRAST AND DYNAMICS: THE SPICE OF LIFE

- Engagement: Use the Five Stage Languages—Pitch, Pace, Punch, Pause, and Passion—to add some zing to your storytelling, like adding jalapenos to your narrative nachos.

Ask yourself: Is my story delivery flatter than a pancake, or more dynamic than a roller coaster?

Remember, folks, this isn't just a checklist—it's your ticket to storytelling stardom. Use it wisely, and you'll craft tales that stick faster than gum on a hot sidewalk.

And hey, if you're sitting there thinking, "Wow, this is great, but I need *more!*"... well, you're in luck. This is just the preview. For the full behind-the-scenes director's commentary, insider tips, and narrative special effects, keep an eye out for my upcoming book and course. It is like film school for your mouth, minus the student loans and pretentious berets.

Now, go forth and direct some narrative blockbusters. Your audience is waiting, and the popcorn's getting cold!

DELETED SCENES: THE TRANSFORMATIONAL NARRATIVE

(OR HOW TO MAKE YOUR SPEECH SO CAPTIVATING, PEOPLE FORGET TO CHECK THEIR PHONES)

> *"All the world's a stage, and all the men and women merely players; they have their exits and entrances."*
>
> **— William Shakespeare, As You Like It**

This is the Transformational Narrative—the storytelling equivalent of a triple espresso shot for your speeches. It isn't just a framework; it's a freaking superpower that'll turn your words into catalysts for change.

Psst: There is a great training available on this over at: **www.mikeganino.com/appendix**

WHY TRANSFORMATION? BECAUSE NOBODY CAME TO YOUR TALK FOR A NAP

Let's face it: the last time a purely informational speech changed someone's life was... never. People don't want information; they want transformation. They want to leave your talk feeling like they've just had a mental makeover, complete with a brain facial and a perspective pedicure.

The Transformational Narrative is your backstage pass to creating that kind of impact. It is a three-act structure designed to take your audience on a journey so compelling, they'll forget to check their phones. (I know, miracle, right?)

ACT 1: SETTING THE STAGE (AKA "YOU ARE HERE")

This is where you prove you're not just another talking head. You are a mind-reader who gets your audience better than their own mother.

The New Shift:

- Hold up a mirror to your audience's current reality.
- Make them nod so hard they risk whiplash.
- What's the current reality your audience is facing?
- What's changed recently in their world?
- Ask yourself:
    - What's keeping my audience up at night?
    - What's the elephant in the room everyone sees but no one talks about?

The Old Story:

- Highlight what's changed.
- Make them realize their old ways are as useful as a chocolate teapot.
- How have things changed?
- What used to work that doesn't anymore?
- Ask yourself:
    - What outdated beliefs or practices does my audience cling to?
    - What's the "We've always done it this way," mentality that needs shaking up?

The "I Want" Song:

- Channel your inner Disney princess and belt out your audience's deepest desires. (Metaphorically. Please don't actually sing unless that's your thing.)
- What does your audience truly desire?
- What's their ultimate goal?
- Ask yourself:
    - If my audience could wave a magic wand, what would they wish for?
    - What's the dream they're afraid to admit even to themselves?

Pro Tip: Start with a bang! Open with something so surprising, your audience forgets they were planning to nap through your talk. "Who wants to get high?" works wonders. (On attention spans, folks. Get your mind out of the gutter.)

ACT 2: THE JOURNEY AND THE OBSTACLES (OR "WHY YOUR AUDIENCE'S CURRENT APPROACH SUCKS")

Now that you've got them hooked, take them on a roller-coaster ride of revelation.

The False Idol:

- Expose the lies they've been sold. It is like telling them Santa isn't real, but for grown-ups.
- What misconceptions or ineffective solutions is your audience currently pursuing?
- Ask yourself:
    - What's the snake oil my audience has been sold?
    - What quick fixes or band-aid solutions are they relying on?

The Promise Land:

- Show them the light at the end of the tunnel. (Spoiler: It's not a train.)
- Who or what exemplifies the success your audience is seeking?
- Ask yourself:
    - Who's already achieved what my audience wants?
    - What case studies or examples can I use to show that success is possible?

The Magic Elixir:

- Drop your big idea like it's hot. This is your "Aha!" moment, your "Eureka!" in the bathtub, your apple falling on Newton's head.
- What's your big idea or solution?
- How will it change everything for your audience?
- Ask yourself:
    - What paradigm shift am I proposing?
    - How can I present my idea so it feels both revolutionary and achievable?

ACT 3: THE CLIMAX AND THE NEW WORLD (AKA "HERE'S HOW YOU ACTUALLY DO THE THING")

Time to turn that revelation into a revolution.

Framework:

- Give them a roadmap so clear, even someone with the sense of direction of a drunk squirrel could follow it.
- What actionable steps or principles can you provide to implement your big idea?
- Ask yourself:
    - How can I break down my solution into digestible, actionable chunks?
    - What's the step-by-step guide my audience needs?

Ultimate Challenge:

- Prepare them for the boss battle. Life isn't a walk in the park; it's more like a sprint through a minefield.
- What obstacles might your audience face when implementing your solution?
- Ask yourself:
    - What's going to trip my audience up when they try this?
    - How can I prepare them for the inevitable setbacks and challenges?

Kingdom is Brighter:

- Paint a picture of success so vivid, they can practically taste it. (Warning: May cause excessive motivation and spontaneous action-taking.)
- What does success look like after implementing your solution?

- Ask yourself:
    - How will my audience's life/work/world be different after they've done what I suggest?
    - What's the before-and-after picture I want to paint?

This framework isn't about filling in the blanks. Dive deep into each element, really understand your audience, and craft a narrative that resonates on a profound level.

Pro Tip: As you work through these steps, keep asking yourself, "So what?" after each point. This will help you dig deeper and ensure every element of your narrative packs a punch.

And hey, if you're thinking, "Wow, this is amazing, but I want *more!*"... you're in luck. This is just the tip of the iceberg—if you want more help, check out my Transformational Narrative training www.mikeganino.com/appendix. (Shameless plug? You bet. But it's like steroids for your speeches—minus the weird side effects.)

Want my 5-Week Keynote From Scratch Developmental Plan? It's waiting for you at: www.mikeganino.com/appendix

BACKSTAGE PASS: INSIDER SECRETS FOR SPEECHCRAFT MASTERY

My speech Scorseses, it's time for some insider tips that'll take your talks from direct-to-DVD to box office gold. Grab your metaphorical director's chair and let's dive in.

The Art of the Open: Cold Opens vs. Warm Opens

Listen up, because this might just blow your mind: nobody came to your talk to hear you clear your throat for five minutes. Shocking, I know.

COLD OPENS: THE JAMES BOND OF SPEECH STARTS

Want to know why James Bond films start with action? Because it works, baby! A cold open in speechmaking is like starting your talk in the middle of a car chase. It grabs attention faster than free pizza at a college dorm.

- Why it works: Your audience is immediately enrolled in a story. Their brains light up like a Christmas tree, and suddenly, they're too engaged to remember they were planning to check their emails.
- How to do it: Jump straight into a vivid story or a provocative question. Save the "Thank you for having me" for your mom's dinner parties.

WARM OPENS: THE COMFY SWEATER OF SPEECHES

Sometimes, you need to ease your audience in gently. A warm open is like inviting them to sit by the fire while you pour them a cup of narrative tea.

- Why it works: It builds rapport and sets the tone. It is great when you need to establish credibility or create a specific mood.
- How to do it: Start with a relevant anecdote, a thoughtful observation, or a question that gets the audience nodding along.

Pro Tip: Whether you go hot or cold, never, ever start with, "Today, I'm going to talk about..." Unless you want your audience to immediately start planning their grocery lists.

The Encore Close: Because Endings Matter, Dammit

Ever been to a concert where the band's best song comes after the fake "goodbye"? That, my friends, is the power of the encore close.

Why it's genius:

1. It gives you control over the final impression.
2. It lets you end on a high note, not on Uncle Bob's rambling question about your slide fonts.

How to nail it:

1. Craft a mini-close before Q&A. It is like the appetizer of endings.
2. Handle Q&A like a boss.
3. Then BAM! Hit 'em with your showstopper close. This is your mic drop moment.

Energy Control: Conducting Your Audience's Buzz

Want a standing ovation? Want your audience buzzing like they've just mainlined espresso? It's all about energy control, baby.

The secret sauce:

1. Pacing: Start slow, build momentum, like a rollercoaster—you gotta go up before you can whoosh down.
2. Cadence: Vary your speech rhythm. Monotony is the enemy of enthusiasm.
3. Energy crescendo: Build to a climax. Your energy should be infectious by the end.

Pro Tip: Practice your close until it flows like butter. The last sixty seconds of your speech should feel like the finale of a fireworks show—all the good stuff, rapid-fire, leaving your audience in awe.

Remember, storytellers extraordinaire, these are the tricks that separate the amateurs from the A-listers. Master these, and you'll have your audience eating out of the palm of your hand.

Now go forth and craft narratives so powerful, they'll make Shakespeare jealous. Your audience is waiting for a story to rock their world. Give it to them.

DELETED SCENES: THE ART OF RHETORIC: WORDPLAYERS GONNA PLAY, PLAY, PLAY, PLAY, PLAY

(OR HOW TO MAKE YOUR WORDS AS CATCHY AS A TAYLOR SWIFT BRIDGE)

THE POWER OF LANGUAGE IN STORYTELLING

Words are more than just a means to an end; they are the building blocks of connection, the threads that weave together our stories, and the instruments that stir emotion and provoke thought. In this appendix, you'll explore various rhetorical devices and wordplay techniques that can elevate your communication from ordinary to extraordinary.

RHYTHM AND REPETITION

Anaphora: The Art of Repetition

Anaphora is the repetition of a word or phrase at the beginning of successive clauses or sentences. This powerful rhetorical device creates a rhythm that can hypnotize an audience, driving home key points through the sheer force of repetition. Anaphora works because it taps into the way our brains process information. The repetition creates a pattern that's easy for our minds to latch on to, making the message more memorable and impactful.

Audiences love anaphora because it provides a sense of structure and builds anticipation. Each repetition reinforces the main idea while adding new information, creating a crescendo effect that can be deeply moving or powerfully motivating. It is particularly effective in speeches or writing that aim to inspire, persuade, or evoke strong emotions.

Use anaphora when you want to emphasize a particular point, create a strong emotional response, or build to a powerful conclusion. It is especially useful in motivational speeches, political addresses, or any situation where you need to rally people around a central idea or call to action.

> **Political Example:** Martin Luther King Jr.'s "I Have a Dream" speech is perhaps the most famous use of anaphora in modern oratory. The repetition of "I have a dream" builds a crescendo of hope and vision.
>
> **Pop Culture Example:** In Taylor Swift's "Should've Said No," she uses anaphora to emphasize regret and consequences: "You should've said no, you should've gone home. You should've thought twice 'fore you let it all go."

Action:

Write a short paragraph about a passion of yours, using anaphora to emphasize key points. Try to emulate the emotional build-up found in King's or Swift's use of the device.

Metaphors: Bridging Ideas With Imagery

Metaphors are figures of speech that describe an object or action in a way that isn't literally true, but helps explain an idea or make a comparison. They aren't just poetic flourishes; metaphors are fundamental to how we understand and experience the world. They allow us to grasp abstract or complex ideas by relating them to concrete, familiar concepts.

The power of metaphors lies in their ability to create instant understanding and emotional connection. When we encounter a well-crafted metaphor, our brains light up, making connections and creating vivid mental images. This not only makes the idea more comprehensible but also more memorable and impactful.

Audiences love metaphors because they make abstract ideas tangible and relatable. A good metaphor can simplify complex concepts, evoke emotions, and create lasting impressions. They are particularly effective when introducing new or challenging ideas, as they provide a familiar framework for understanding.

Use metaphors when you need to explain complex or abstract concepts, when you want to make an emotional impact, or when you're trying to make your message more memorable. They are especially useful in educational settings, motivational speeches, and when discussing abstract concepts like love, time, or success.

> **TED Talk Example:** In his talk "Do schools kill creativity?", Sir Ken Robinson uses the metaphor of mining to describe education: "We have to go into the mind of the child... Our education system has mined our minds in the way that we strip-mine the earth: for a particular commodity."
>
> **Political Example:** Barack Obama often used the "ship of state" metaphor during his 2008 campaign, casting himself as the captain who would steer America through turbulent waters.

Action:

> Take an abstract concept (like love, success, or time) and create three different metaphors to explain it. Then, try to use one in a mini-speech, emulating Robinson's or Obama's style.

The Rule of Three: Tricolon and Isocolon

The rule of three is a writing principle suggesting that things that come in threes are inherently more satisfying and effective than other numbers of things. This principle manifests in rhetoric through devices like tricolon (a series of three parallel elements) and isocolon (three elements of equal length and structure).

The power of three works because it creates a pattern that's short enough to remember, but long enough to create rhythm. It satisfies our natural tendency to look for patterns and creates a sense of completeness. In a tricolon, the third element often provides emphasis or a climactic ending, while an isocolon creates a pleasing balance.

Audiences respond well to the rule of three because it's familiar (think "The Three Little Pigs" or *The Good, the Bad, and the Ugly*) and easy to remember. It creates a rhythm that's pleasing to the ear and helps structure information in a way that feels natural and complete.

Use the rule of three when you want to emphasize key points, create a memorable phrase, or structure your entire speech or presentation. It is particularly effective in slogans, persuasive speeches, and when you want to create a sense of completeness or inevitability.

> **Tricolon Example (rising intensity):** From Julius Caesar, "I came, I saw, I conquered." (Veni, vidi, vici)
>
> **Isocolon Example:** From Abraham Lincoln's Gettysburg Address, "Government of the people, by the people, for the people."

Pop Culture Example: In *The Hunger Games*, the rebellion's rallying cry is a perfect tricolon: "If we burn, you burn with us!"

Action:

Create a tricolon to describe a personal achievement, with each element building in intensity. Then, craft an isocolon to describe a product or service you're passionate about.

Captatio Benevolentiae: Winning Goodwill

Captatio benevolentiae, which literally means "capturing goodwill" in Latin, is a rhetorical technique used to gain the audience's favor right from the start of a speech or piece of writing. It is about establishing a connection, showing humility, and aligning yourself with your audience's values or emotions.

This technique works because it breaks down barriers between the speaker and the audience. By showing vulnerability, relatability, or shared experiences, the speaker creates an instant rapport. It extends a friendly handshake before diving into the meat of the conversation.

Audiences love captatio benevolentiae because it makes them feel seen, understood, and valued. It transforms the speech from a one-way monologue into a conversation between friends. This technique is particularly effective in situations where you need to overcome skepticism, address a potentially hostile audience, or simply create a warm, receptive atmosphere.

Use captatio benevolentiae at the beginning of your speech or writing, especially when you're addressing a new audience, tackling a controversial topic, or when you need to quickly establish trust and credibility.

> **TED Talk Example:** Brené Brown opens her famous talk on vulnerability by saying:
>
> So, I'll start with this: a couple years ago, an event planner called me because I was going to do a speaking event. And she called, and she said, "I'm really struggling with how to write about you on the little flyer." And I thought, "Well, what's the struggle?" And she said, "Well, I saw you speak, and I'm going to call you a researcher, I think, but I'm afraid if I call you a researcher, no one will come, because they'll think you're boring and irrelevant."
>
> This opening immediately establishes Brown as relatable and self-deprecating, winning the audience's goodwill.

Action:

Draft an opening paragraph for a speech that uses captatio benevolentiae to connect with your audience immediately. Try to emulate Brown's style of using a personal anecdote that relates to the audience's potential perceptions.

Praeteritio: The Art of Mentioning by Not Mentioning

Praeteritio is a rhetorical device where the speaker or writer brings up a subject by stating that it will not be discussed. It is a clever way of highlighting information while pretending to pass over it.

This technique works because it plays on the psychological principle of reactance—the idea that people tend to do or think about the very thing they're told not to. By saying you won't mention something, you're actually drawing attention to it. It is also effective because it can make the audience feel like they're being let in on a secret or given information that others might miss.

Audiences find praeteritio intriguing because it creates a sense of complicity between the speaker and listener. It can add a touch of humor, irony, or emphasis to a speech. It is particularly effective when you want to bring up a point without dwelling on it, or when you want to mention something potentially controversial while maintaining plausible deniability.

Use praeteritio when you want to emphasize a point without explicitly stating it, when you want to bring up a sensitive topic indirectly, or when you want to add a touch of wit or irony to your speech. It is especially useful in debates, political speeches, or any situation where direct statements might be too blunt or controversial.

Political Example: In his "Checkers" speech, Richard Nixon uses praeteritio when he says, "I don't believe I ought to quit because I'm not a quitter. And, incidentally, Pat's not a quitter. After all, her name was

Patricia Ryan and she was born on St. Patrick's Day, and you know the Irish never quit."

Pop Culture Example: In *Hamilton*, the song "Election of 1800" uses praeteritio when Burr sings, "I don't like Adams... Well, he's going to lose, that's just defeatist."

Action:

Write a short paragraph about a controversial topic, using praeteritio to subtly highlight key points without directly addressing them.

Rhetorical Questions: Engaging the Audience's Mind

Rhetorical questions are questions asked for effect or to emphasize a point, rather than to elicit an answer. They prompt the audience to think about the answer, engaging them more deeply with the topic at hand.

This technique works because it activates the audience's mind, encouraging them to participate mentally in the speech. Instead of passively receiving information, listeners are prompted to think, reflect, and come to their own conclusions. This increased engagement often leads to better retention of the information and a stronger emotional connection to the message.

Audiences appreciate rhetorical questions because they break the monotony of declarative statements and create a sense of dialogue, even in a monologue setting. They can also create dramatic effect, emphasize a point, or lead the audience to a desired conclusion.

Use rhetorical questions when you want to engage your audience more actively, when you're building up to an important point, or when you want to challenge your listeners' assumptions. They are particularly effective in persuasive speeches, debates, and when you want to create a moment of reflection or emphasis.

> **TED Talk Example:** In her talk "The Power of Vulnerability," Brené Brown asks, "How do we learn to embrace our vulnerabilities and imperfections so that we can engage in our lives from a place of authenticity and worthiness? How do we cultivate the courage, compassion, and connection that we need to recognize that we are enough—that we are worthy of love, belonging, and joy?"

Action:

Take a section of your story or speech and add one or two rhetorical questions. Practice delivering them with different vocal techniques—slow down the pace to give your audience time to reflect, or punch a key question with emphasis to command attention.

By mastering these rhetorical devices, you'll craft messages that not only inform but inspire, persuade, and leave a lasting impact on your audience. The goal is not to use these devices for their own sake, but to enhance your authentic voice and message. As you practice, you'll find ways to weave these techniques into your natural speaking style, creating a more powerful and engaging presence in all your communications.

THE ART OF WORDPLAY AS A TOOL FOR AUTHENTIC EXPRESSION

Remember, these techniques are tools to enhance your natural communication style, not to replace it. The most powerful communication comes from authenticity, with these devices serving to amplify your message and connect more deeply with your audience.

Final Action:

> Write a short speech (two or three minutes) on a topic you're passionate about. Incorporate at least five of the rhetorical devices we've discussed. Practice delivering it, focusing on how these techniques enhance your natural speaking style.

By mastering these rhetorical devices and incorporating them thoughtfully into your communication, you can craft messages that not only inform but inspire, persuade, and leave a lasting impact on your audience.